They call it "God's story book"—translation of the Bible into a native language. For forty-five amazing years, Bob and Mariel Ward joyfully devoted their lives to the work of Bible translation on the Philippine island of Mindanao. Mariel, a natural storyteller, recounts in riveting detail how throughout those years God abundantly provided for all their needs, directed their steps, and protected them as they lived simply on His promises. In their years of unwavering commitment to the call of God, Bob and Mariel witnessed the outpouring of the Holy Spirit through miracles, healings, and changed lives. God opened door after door for them in spite of seemingly insurmountable obstacles, including death threats by the *imams*, animistic beliefs, demonic activity, and serious illness. Their unwavering work among the Maranao people will encourage and challenge any reader who is considering a ministry in missions, as well as anyone desiring a deeper walk of faith and trust in the Lord. A must-read!

—Kathy Treece
CRISTA Missionary Service

What an amazing and dramatic story Mariel Ward tells about the life she and her husband, Bob, lived among the Maranao people of the Philippines, and their commitment both to the people and to the task of translating the Bible into the Maranao language. Not only did they have to learn the language "from scratch" and reduce it to writing, they had to learn how to translate biblical words and concepts into the vernacular, which the Maranao people could easily understand. And all the while they were raising four children in primitive conditions, demonstrating the love and power of God as they translated and healed sicknesses and preached the gospel, often in the midst of their own physical weakness and suffering.

But the major obstacle to the lifelong task God had called them to was that the Maranaos are Muslims. They have been Muslims for more than four hundred years—and so fiercely that the idea of the Bible in their own language produced death threats from the *imams* and village leaders, making it necessary for the Wards to keep a very low profile for many years. One must often read between the lines to determine the pressures such a way of life put on Bob and Mariel. But one does not have to read between the lines to learn what sustained them through these years and brought them to a successful accomplishment of their calling. It has been the power of God through the presence of the Holy Spirit, producing miracles, giving direction and wisdom as well as joy and delight. And now the complete Bible is in the Maranao language and is posted on the Web.

—Mary Ruth Howes
Retired editor, Guideposts Books

Penetrating the Stronghold of Islam

An Insider's Perspective *from a* Bible Translation Team

Mariel Ward

Creation House

Penetrating the Stronghold of Islam by Mariel Ward

Published by Creation House

A Charisma Media Company

600 Rinehart Road

Lake Mary, Florida 32746

www.charismamedia.com

Unless otherwise noted, all scripture quotations are from the King James version.

Cover design by Rachel Campbell

Library of Congress Control Number: 2008937223

International Standard Book Number: 978-1-59979-486-0

Author's note: Names have been changed to protect identities.

13 14 15 16 — 12 11 10 9 8

Printed in the United States of America

To Bob, my best friend

Contents

Chapter 1

Year of Decision

Stony Brook

How would you like to start training with Wycliffe this summer?" Bob asked as he walked in the door after a day of teaching.

It was 1959 and we were four years into our marriage, asking the Lord to make this our year of decision. We needed a definite call. Whether we ended up in secular work or Christian ministry was not the issue. We wanted to know God's plan for our lives. To stay on Long Island at the Stony Brook School for Boys would be sheer joy. The Lord had blessed us with two little ones, Greig and Carole, and a beautiful home in which to raise them. There was ample room for four more, and that was our plan. It also had an expansive yard where Monty, our devoted Great Pyrenees, was serious about his responsibility of watching over our burgeoning family. Bob had transformed the basement into an enviable recreation room, complete with a ping-pong table and two of his handsomely carved box-hockey sets. I wanted to live and die in that house.

Saturday nights after dinner in the school dining hall, we would ask our table of boys what their plans were for the evening. All eight would invariably chorus, "Nothing," with a hopeful shrug.

"Well, come on over," we'd tell them.

Our house was across the street from campus, and after tucking the babies in bed, I would pop a cake in the oven and put on the hot chocolate. We did indeed have a ministry with the boys, but we wanted the Lord to make it clear to us whether He wanted this to be a permanent one. Was this what He had planned for us to do the rest of our lives, and if not, what then? We were not content to drift along in His permissive will.

By divine coincidence, we were reading missionary biographies that year. Betty Elliot's books had just come off the press, and Pete Fleming, one of the five missionaries who were killed by the Auca Indians of Ecuador, had been a friend of Bob's. They had played church basketball together during university days in Seattle. Books from my parents' library, like *Reese Howells: Intercessor*, were also among our reading, and by February we had received the Reader's Digest condensation of *Two Thousand Tongues to Go*, by Ethel Wallis. It was the story of Wycliffe Bible Translators and their frontier missionary efforts to provide Bibles for tribes, that did not yet have a Bible in their own language.

Laying the magazine down on the coffee table one morning, I looked up. "Lord," I prayed, "if by any chance You want us to train with Wycliffe this summer, please have Bob bring up the subject without my mentioning it."

I knew the Lord was more than able to do that; I just didn't expect Him to do it so quickly! When Bob walked in from school that very afternoon and asked me how I would feel about training with Wycliffe that summer, I said, "Just a minute," and called the real estate agent to put our house on the market. Why wait? The Lord's answer was clear.

What I did not know that day was that a number of years before we met, Bob had committed his life to the Lord specifically for the work of Bible translation. Like the other men in his family, he had graduated from the University of Washington with a degree in electrical engineering. Sometime during his senior year he attended a spiritual retreat where he was challenged to surrender his life completely to the Lord. He responded after graduation by enrolling in Dallas Theological Seminary, where he majored in Greek and Hebrew for four years. His express purpose was to prepare himself for translating the Bible from the original Hebrew and Greek texts into an unwritten dialect, a formidable challenge indeed. During Bob's last year of seminary, Dr. Frank Gaebelein taught a module, as he did each spring. One of his primary objectives in being there was to recruit seminary graduates for teaching at his boys' prep school on Long Island. Still a bachelor with no plans for marriage on the horizon, Bob accepted the invitation in 1953 and became the math and Bible teacher at the Stony Brook Boys School, as it was known then.

We Meet

We met two years later. I was teaching English at a prep school in Brooklyn while preparing for a campus ministry with InterVarsity. Bob and I were introduced while chaperoning our respective students at a conference in the lovely, snow-capped Pocono Mountains of Pennsylvania.

"And *who* needed the chaperone?" my students asked when we announced our engagement the following month.

My missionary parents balked. Our plans were unfolding too fast for them. A month before school was out for the summer, however, the Lord spoke to Mother and assured her that He was in charge. From that moment on, because of my heavy teaching schedule and because I was living in Brooklyn while we were to be married in New Jersey, Mother handled all the wedding plans. We simply showed up for the wedding when school was out in June and left directly afterward for a two-week honeymoon trip to Seattle, where Bob took a summer job and I got acquainted with my new family.

It was during his six years of teaching at Stony Brook that Bob temporarily lost the vision for Bible translation. We were busy making babies and settling into our nest, and the subject of missions never came up. That is, not until we read *Two Thousand Tongues to Go*. God can use even the Reader's Digest to speak to His children!

Jungle Camp

One of Wycliffe's basic requirements was three months of jungle training camp in southern Mexico, which included classes in first aid techniques as well as survival training, in which we learned to adapt physically and emotionally to primitive living conditions. By summer of that year we had packed up our babies, loaded our almost-new Chevy station wagon, and were on our way. With two summers of linguistics ahead of us and Jungle Camp sandwiched in-between, we had a full plate. Moreover, I was again "*great* with child."

Keith, who was obviously going to be a large baby, was due after our first summer of linguistic training. During the delivery, my obstetrician placed bets with the nurses on the size of the baby making his debut. He was eleven and one-half pounds. The doctor won the bets, of course.

Before leaving for Mexico, we happened to be visiting with a member of the Philippine branch of Wycliffe who was home on furlough. When he heard we were leaving for Jungle Camp with three babies, he questioned our sanity! By the time we arrived in Mexico, we were wondering the same thing. Keith was under three months old when we left Seattle.

When the road ended down near the Guatemala border, we parked our car at the missionary aviation base and flew the rest of the way into Mexico's virgin jungle, where we would literally make our home for the next three months.

Here Bob built a *champa*, which is a thatched roof shelter without walls. As required, he built it without any materials at all except what he could glean with his machete from the jungle, like bamboo, and vines with which to tie the bamboo poles. With these he made a table and a platform for our sleeping bags, the edge of which served as dining room bench. Above the bed he made a "loft"—a shelf where he secured two jungle hammocks for a two and three-year-old. He constructed a mud stove, drew all our water from the river, and cut firewood for cooking, while I cared for a newborn and attempted to keep two very young children from falling into the nearby churning river. By the time we arrived in Mexico, I had still not regained my strength after delivering such a large baby. Without God's help on an hourly basis, we would never have made it. Sharon, number four, was born several years later under entirely different circumstances.

Years after jungle camp, during our early days of pioneer living, we were to be profoundly grateful for our Spartan training as we watched one family after another from other missions attempt work among our people, only to abandon the effort within a few months or a year. Unfortunately, this was without exception.

Financial Support

It was just after our first summer of linguistics, that the question of support came up. "If God can't take care of us, why are we going to the other side of the world to tell people how great He is?" was our naïve stance. We knew only that back in those early years Wycliffe did not require its members to raise a given quota for monthly support. If we wished to go out and starve, that was our prerogative. That policy would change in time.

A couple from our Baptist church in Tacoma were taking the same linguistic course with us at the University of Washington in order to improve their language skills when they returned to Africa for a second term. They told us about the plans they had made to drive across the country that fall, speaking in churches all along the way. They needed to raise their support level before their Baptist mission would allow them to return to the field, so they had arranged a heavy schedule of speaking as they traveled to New York, where they would board their flight back to Africa.

"You mean you are going to be speaking in churches just to get money?" we asked incredulously.

We were worse than naïve—we were completely ignorant of the practices of "faith" missions. As we pondered this question of God's ability to take care of us, we first had to settle the issue of pride. Were we too proud to do what our friends were doing? Was raising support too humbling? Finally, we told the Lord we were willing to do anything He required of us as long as He made it perfectly clear, and we meant it. Our Baptist church in Tacoma gave a substantial monthly allowance to all its missionaries, so we could at least count on that.

One week before the summer was over, we received our first check through Wycliffe. It was from a couple whom we had never met or heard of. The check was in the amount of twenty-five dollars, not much today, but it was pure gold in 1959. It had apparently floated straight down from heaven, and through it God was saying, "I can indeed take care of you!" The message came through loud and clear.

The interesting thing was that we had no need of money that summer. We were in the process of selling our Long Island home and had taken in a handsome sum from our garage sale before we left. Later we learned from whence this currency from heaven had come. Don, a colleague of Bob's at Stony Brook, married that summer just after we left, and his new in-laws, the Watts, were looking for a way to support the work of Bible translation. They preferred, however, to give to an individual Bible translator rather than to the general mission fund, so Don told them about Bob.

What is more amazing is that for forty-five long years this well never ran dry, and we continued to be blessed by that first couple. When the husband died a number of years later, we were not expecting his widow to continue the monthly support, which had increased substantially over the years. But she never missed a beat. Some years later, when she joined her husband in heaven, we thanked God for this wonderful couple who had meant so much to us, never dreaming that one of their daughters would continue their ministry of giving.

"I'm not going to miss out on this blessing," their daughter Carolyn wrote as she picked up her parents' monthly support for us and continued for the remainder of our forty-five years in the Philippines!

What most profoundly impacted us is the incredible faithfulness of our loving God, who has never yet broken a promise.

There is more to this matter of support. After that first summer was behind us, as well as jungle camp and another summer of linguistics, we were finally ready to set sail for the Philippines with three children, four years old and under. The night before our departure, the deacons of our church threw an elegant farewell party for us. At the end of a delightful evening, two of the deacons walked us to the door. As they said good-bye, the head deacon spoke: "Bob and Mariel, we love you very much, but we have a policy in our church, 'Baptist money for Baptist missions.'"

We smiled feebly as we said goodnight. If a horse had kicked us in the stomach, it could not have been more painful. We walked slowly to our car, with the realization that we would be leaving the shores of America the following day with *no promised support*! We had no assurance at that time that even the twenty-five dollars from the Watts would continue on a regular basis. Stepping onto the gangplank in Seattle the next day as people of great faith and power, we said to no one in particular, "If God lets us down, we'll just go home!"

For the first two years we lived entirely in the village, where our needs were minimal, as was our income. The third year, however, found us assigned to Manila, where the cost of living more than doubled. Because I am Rh-negative and was expecting our fourth baby, it was imperative for me to deliver in Manila. No doctor on Mindanao wanted anything to do with me, ill-equipped as they were to deal with a complete transfusion for the newborn, should the Rh factor create that need. This was 1963, before the days of Rh-immune globulin injections. At the same time, Bob was asked to fill the position of Manila buyer to respond to the needs of translators in remote areas.

Although we had no idea ahead of time that we would need twice as much income to survive in the big city, the Lord knew all about it, and that is exactly what we received from the moment we landed in Manila. Our income more than doubled until the end of the year, when it dropped back to half the amount for the last month. The Lord was obviously saying, "It's time to return to the barrio!" For forty-five years there would always be enough. We did not know from month to month where it would come from, but we were getting to know the One from whom it comes!

The Philippines

It was mostly selfish motives that led us to choose the Philippines for our country of ministry. English is the medium of instruction in that country and is therefore widely used, which meant we were not required to learn the trade language first but could proceed directly to the dialect in which we would be translating. And there were many of these language groups without a translation of the Bible. Furthermore, having been born and raised in China, I was eager to get as close to my roots as possible, and the Philippines was the closest country. China was closed, and none of the other Asian branches of Wycliffe had opened up yet.

On May 2, 1961, our American Mail Lines freighter dropped anchor in Manila Bay after four long weeks at sea. We disembarked with hands firmly grasping three small children and our hearts filled with thrilled expectancy. As we stepped off the gangplank onto Philippine soil, we had a sense of awe and wonderment, of hopes and dreams about to be fulfilled, and enough youthful self-confidence to conquer the islands for Jesus.

A few days later we were on our way down to Nasuli on the southern island of Mindanao, home to Wycliffe's only base in the Philippines at that time. With a spring-fed natural swimming hole and many hectares of open land, Nasuli was a child's paradise, where children were free to roam the fields or camp out under a mango tree. There was also ample room for an airstrip, which would soon be needed. Located in the very center of Mindanao, Nasuli provided the idyllic backdrop for translation teams to come out of their allocations for workshops, seminars, extended periods of uninterrupted work, as well as vacations.

Assignment

When the director asked us what tribal group we felt drawn to, we chorused, "Wherever we're needed most."

He then outlined the three areas that were top priority. To reach either the first or second, we would have multiple river crossings. In fact, we would have to cross seven rivers to reach the first one. Travel to both of these language groups was considered too dangerous for a family with three little ones. The third area, however, could be reached by land, even though the road was not more than a cow path. It was the consensus, therefore, that the land route would be better for us than numerous river crossings with three small children. Losing a baby in the river is never a good thing.

And so it was that we joyfully accepted our assignment to a large Muslim group, the Maranaos. Bob and I had no premonition when we left the States that we would be working with Muslims. We didn't even know there was a Muslim in the Philippines!

There is further irony in this assignment. During my year of graduate school at Wheaton College, before Bob and I had met, the speaker at our grad school chapel one day was the head of a large mission in Africa whose work was entirely with Muslims. I don't remember a word the speaker had to say, but I distinctly remember my reaction. As we filed out of chapel at the close of the service that morning, I said to the girl next to me, "What a waste!"

As far as I was concerned, it was an exercise in futility to try to reach Muslims for Christ. By the time our training was behind us and our assignment determined, however, the religion of our target people no longer mattered. We had a specific job to do, and we were eager to get started. God would have to do the rest.

Chapter 2

Tugaya on the Shores of Lake Lanao

The Lush Island of Mindanao

There are seven thousand islands in the Philippine archipelago, although less than nine hundred are inhabited. The two largest are Luzon in the north and Mindanao in the south. The northern island is home to the nation's capital, Manila, and to the Tagalog people, whose dialect is the official national language, as well as to the Ilocano.

Although not quite as large as Luzon, Mindanao in the south, along with the Visayan Islands, boasts a far greater population than either of the major groups in the north. The language of this Philippine majority in the south is Visayan.

Insulated by the gentle, untroubled waters of the Philippine Sea, where thousands of islands decorate the horizon, Mindanao is protected from the harsh hurricanes that devastate the north on a regular basis. No more than residual rains reach Mindanao, lasting for a week at a time. Instead of leaving devastation in their wake, these rains serve only to enhance the lush verdure that carpets the mountains and rolling hills of Mindanao, keeping it green all year round.

The Moros

Traveling for two days on an inter-island boat from Manila to Mindanao, one is lulled by the serenity of the seascape and the sublime grandeur of mountains rising from the sea. Stepping off the boat, however, one is soon reminded that Mindanao is home to some seven Muslim ethnic groups. They are easy to spot, especially the women in their colorful circular garment, the *malong,* which is gathered above the bust, although today they are more likely to be hiding behind the black habit and veil of Middle Eastern Muslims, their eyes peeking through a narrow slit.

When we first arrived, these Muslims were disparagingly referred to as *moros*, a term dating back to Spanish rule. The Moors were Muslims who crossed into Spain from North Africa and controlled most of Spain for three centuries. Hence the Spaniards dubbed these Filipino Muslims *moros.* It is these Muslims who have been waging a war of secession for decades. The government has tried various means to appease its troublesome minority, even granting tantalizing measures of autonomy, which has served only to increase demands. Tagalogs in Manila refer to their southern headache as "MuslimMindanao," all one word, as if trying to dismiss a migraine. Far from being Muslim, however, Mindanao is more than 80 percent Catholic Visayan, who are prepared to defend their homeland and culture with their lives. Thus, conflict has been the norm for centuries on the island of Mindanao.

It is the Visayans who have built all the major cities on Mindanao and produced the progress that industry and commerce have achieved, whereas the only city developed entirely by Muslims is Marawi City, whose civilization lags far behind the rest of Mindanao. Visitors are shocked by the contrast. Nevertheless, the Muslim objective is to control the entire island of Mindanao and secede from the nation. No wonder blood has been shed over the struggle for Mindanao.

Since the Spanish conquest of the Philippines in the mid-sixteenth century, Mindanao has been home to the Maranao, one of the largest Muslim groups, now numbering nearly two million, although the government downplays the census of this burgeoning minority. Maranaos have earned the reputation of being the most fanatically Muslim as well as the most pugnacious of all these groups.

The first Arab missionary traders predated Magellan by two centuries and successfully converted a significant number of pagans, promising many wives and easy salvation. Animistic tribes found this new religion appealing, as it guaranteed sensual rewards with easy-to-meet demands. All one had to do was recite a simple creed, pray briefly five times a day, give an occasional coin to a beggar, fast for the month of Ramadan (which is really feasting at night), and make a pilgrimage to Mecca—but don't worry if you can't make it.

Lake Lanao

When the Spaniards first arrived, Muslim sultanates ruled in Manila but soon fled to the rugged jungles of Mindanao, where Spain never succeeded in conquering or converting them, a fact for which the Maranao is rightly proud. In fleeing before Spain, Maranaos marked out the choicest spot on Mindanao, both in beauty and climate. They settled in the cool air of a majestic mountain range with a sparkling lake nestled in its lap. Ten miles long and five miles wide, Lake Lanao lies in the crater of an ancient volcano half a mile above sea level with a raging river plunging twenty miles to the ocean. The word for lake in Maranao is *ranao,* or as it is pronounced in Visayan, *lanao.* Thus Lake Lanao literally means "Lake Lake" and lends its name to its home province, Lanao del Sur. Maranaos used to refer to themselves as People of the Lake.

Marawi City, the provincial capital, sits forbiddingly at the head of the lake, blanketed in spiritual oppression that has erupted in recent decades into widespread kidnappings. It has seen a deluge of Muslim extremists, bringing terrorism from the Middle East. Today it is offlimits to visitors, especially whites, making it a forbidden city, indeed. Maranao barrios cluster tightly around the lake with their hundreds of mosques decorating the shore, gold-colored domes shimmering in the sunlight. Against a backdrop of majestic mountains rising from its depths, the water reflects azure skies, while supplying ample water for ceremonial ablutions. To the uninitiated, the breathtaking panoramic beauty deceivingly veils the pollution of the world's largest latrine, which sparkles clear while hiding the pain of cholera and typhoid epidemics. Its multi-purpose water is used for drinking, bathing, defecating, fishing, laundry, and the ceremonial cleansing and pre-burial washing of corpses, epidemic victims and all. Swimming soon loses its lure for all but the locals.

It was to these proud and colorful Maranaos that Dr. Frank Laubach devoted years of service in the 1930's and where he launched his world-acclaimed literacy movement, Each One Teach One. His ministry claimed three converts, albeit cultural conversions. It was for these followers of Muhammad that we were assigned to translate the Bible.

Tugaya

As soon as our assignment was confirmed, Bob and our director made a motorcycle run to Marawi City to determine the best place for our family to locate. Government officials unanimously recommended the barrio of Tugaya, and once we were settled there, we learned why. Tugaya had the worst reputation of any place around the lake, home to a record number of outlaws, and the provincial government was hoping to improve that image by the presence of an American family! Nevertheless, this was the heart of Maranao culture, and we would forever be profoundly grateful for the opportunity to saturate ourselves with the language and customs in this strategic area, which before long was off-limits to outsiders. The entire area would soon be closed behind the pale of Islam.

So it was that we arrived in the barrio of Tugaya one steamy afternoon with our five duffle bags and three small children, only to find that the house for which Bob had negotiated was bulging with occupants. Furthermore, the landlord had no intention of evicting anyone and assumed we would become part of his overcrowded household as his long-term guests. Although this arrangement didn't appeal to us, it would soon be dark, and we wondered where we would bed down our little ones that night.

Finally, a very short man by the name of Galgal came to our rescue. He was the son of the sultan and had a brother, Hadji Abdullah, who was away at the time but who had an unfinished house that we could rent, an offer we jumped at. Although there were four families living downstairs, including the landlord's, we would have the privacy of the crude upstairs, which was a large open hall under a tin roof, not sealed off by a ceiling. Each family below us slept on one hard, oversized kapok mattress on the floor, separated from the next by a thin curtain which was drawn aside during the day.

Our new home was farther down the dusty mountain trail, and we followed the narrow path slowly toward the lake while the children tried to keep up with our pace. The people helped us up the ladder with our duffle bags, and then the entire barrio, it seemed, crowded in to watch us get settled. They brought generous bowls of steaming rice for our supper and water to slake our thirst. We ate sitting on the floor and drank without caution while angels purified our drinking water.

For three days we lived with crowds of people watching our every move until, at the end of the third day, my taut nerves snapped and I collapsed in a faint. Galgal was immediately solicitous. He was a schoolteacher and knew a little English.

"What's wrong with Missus?" he asked.

Bob explained, mostly with gestures, that he thought I had been overcome by the stress of so many people constantly around, whereupon Galgal swiftly evicted everyone. We soon learned that our open-door policy needed limits, like mealtimes and personal and family devotions.

The one exception to this rule was our fatherly landlord, Hadji Abdullah, who was fascinated by our custom of sitting on chairs and eating at a table instead of gathering around a brass tray on the floor. We had tried that arrangement without success, with filth from the floor invading our food and an unrestrained toddler free to roam. Hadji Abdullah felt it was his prerogative as our host to squat in a corner and watch us, and we soon got used to his friendly intrusion. Furthermore, he turned out to be my personal language tutor. Though he didn't know a word of English, he would stand beside me when barrio children climbed the ladder to sell a papaya or a squash. As I pointed to a coin or item of food, he would give me the Maranao word and show me what coins to pay, while I wrote down the word phonetically. We had to eat, and the well-being of my family depended on my ability to communicate with these young traders. Under such pressure, vocabulary was easy to absorb.

Maranao Culture

The Maranao method of choice for earning a living is smuggling. Small boats slip in the back door from Indonesia, disgorging contraband goods on the eastern shores of Mindanao, thus avoiding the high import taxes in Manila. Furthermore, when pilgrims return from Mecca each year, it is a given that each will come heavily laden with illegal goods, while the government turns a blind eye, hoping to appease this large, unruly minority.

Because Maranaos have been a proud people since their tribal days, and because of their ill-gotten wealth, they are too proud to work for hire, although many remain poor. With no carpenters available, therefore, Bob put his tools to use immediately and erected partitions for bedrooms, much to the amazement of the people. Privacy was a new concept, but soon neighbors all around us were putting up partitions in their houses! He nailed crude lumber to the walls, which served as open shelves for our few belongings. We tried laying our foam mattresses on the floor in an attempt to live as much like our people as possible, but soon gave this up in favor of cleanliness. Sweeping filth from the floor onto our beds was repugnant, so Bob made wooden platforms for our mattresses.

The day after our arrival, the old sultan promptly adopted us as his son and daughter and promised to slit the throat of anyone who harmed us, demonstrating his intentions with gestures. We found his concern amusing at first, but it wasn't long before we learned to appreciate the protection of this powerful man.

"The only thing I cannot guarantee is your health," the old man apologized as Galgal interpreted, and we readily agreed that he could not be responsible for that.

Visitors filled the large central area of the upstairs during daylight hours. That first week in Tugaya, while Bob was still making bedroom partitions and we were wishing we had a table to eat at, four strong young men came one morning bearing a mammoth table for us. What a wonderful provision from the Lord! It was a rough-hewn square slab, big enough to comfortably accommodate twelve people. It was much too large for our little family, but if one third were cut off, it would provide us with a much-needed kitchen table as well. That evening, when the people had left out of respect for our dinner hour, Bob sawed off a portion of it, leaving us with a perfect-size dining room table, as well as one for the kitchen.

The next morning the people admired the table, our newest display of sophistication. They also seemed pleased that we now had a way to elevate our kerosene stove from the kitchen floor to a better height for us. They had noticed we didn't squat as gracefully as they.

That afternoon, however, the mood changed. Instead of admiring Bob's creativity, there were several men present with somber faces, shaking their heads. Finally we learned that this table was somewhat of a museum relic, and we had destroyed it, or so they claimed! A high ranking princess had died on this table during the powerful earthquake that convulsed the center of the lake the decade before, causing tidal waves, which drowned whole barrios of people along the lakeshore. Still vivid in everyone's memory, earthquake stories abounded when we first arrived. We learned that afternoon that it would take many hundreds of pesos to compensate for the damage done by cutting the valuable table! After much haggling, a large sum was agreed upon, which Bob reluctantly paid. We learned early on to be wary of the devious ways of the Maranao, who are always eager to rise to a financial challenge.

One of our earliest needs was for a toilet. This would require the grueling work of digging a large pit. Bob was elbow-deep in meeting other emergency demands, but with no labor available for hire, we were faced with a crisis, which we decided to discuss with our landlord. To our surprise, Hadji Abdullah promised to get someone to do this work for us. The fee was high but definitely worth it. Imagine our shock when that someone turned out to be a woman! He referred to her as his sister-in-law, which seemed strange to us because both he and his wife were hadjis, having made the *hadj* to Mecca, and therefore enjoyed an elevated status in the community. We kept silent, however, realizing we had much to learn in our new environment, and quietly observed the woman digging for several days under the broiling sun. When she asked for a little cigarette money each day, I gave it, still puzzling over the social order. We got our toilet but without being able to figure out why no men were available for carpentry when a woman was willing to do heavy manual labor.

More than a year later, our eyes were opened. One of the hometown boys returned from law school in Manila, a rare case in the early sixties of a local Maranao making good academically. Sahariman had attended school consistently enough to be able to tackle higher education. While home for a couple of weeks' vacation, he visited us, and as we sat on our porch watching the familiar scenes below, he pointed out various individuals.

"Do you see that man there?" he asked. "He is a slave."

While we recovered from shock, he continued to point out other slaves, both male and female.

"That girl was born to slaves," he said. "Her parents had a kind master who allowed them to marry."

Girls born into slavery, we learned, normally became slave concubines, bringing in a dowry for their owner, though not nearly one as large as a Muslim girl would command.

"But where do these slaves come from?" we queried.

"They are Visayans," Sahariman replied.

And that's when we learned that the Maranao word for "slave" is *visaya!* This explained why Muslims looked down on the rest of the population of Mindanao and its surrounding islands. They are Visayans, and for the "People of the Lake," that term denotes the slave class! Sahariman then told us about the slave raids of previous centuries, which have continued into the present. Maranaos traveled by boat to the surrounding Visayan Islands, capturing women and children unrestrainedly. Every large home in Tugaya has its household slaves, and we soon learned to recognize them.

In the years to come, we were to learn about the Muslim judicial system. If any of these slaves ever tried to escape, there were enough Maranaos around to recapture them and return them to their owners, who then beat them mercilessly. Or, as in the case of a few, when they got as far as Marawi City, they were brought to court, where Muslim lawyers made a mockery of the trial, claiming that the runaways owed enormous sums of money for their years of room, board, and clothing, money which they could never repay in a lifetime.

We also learned later that far from being a practice of yesteryear, the slave trade is alive and well today, though mostly carried out with more sophistication. Traveling Muslim traders make their way to distant corners of the Philippines selling their smuggled goods. Often they come across a poor farmer to whom they will offer a very small dowry for one of his daughters, promising her a better life. Visayans do not practice dowry, so this bride price, though it would never buy a Muslim bride, is an enormous sum to the impoverished farmer who has more mouths to feed than he has food. When the lovely Visayan farmer's daughter arrives on the lake expecting a wedding and a new home, she discovers to her anguish that she is a slave concubine, subject to the often harsh treatment of wife number one or her master. She then has the choice of accepting her lot in life and raising her children to be Muslims or attempting the impossible feat of escape.

This is how we discovered why one of the wives in the

house across from us spoke a little English but was too ashamed of being a slave concubine to explain her status. She was captured from the outlying area of Davao, a large city on the eastern shores of Mindanao. Although we were deeply distressed by what we were learning, it answered many of our questions. Our toilet had been dug by slave labor, and it had taken more than a year for us to realize this!

Playmates

After the incident over our ill-fated dining room table, life settled down to a modicum of normalcy. Our children played with Maranao children and Maulana, our landlord's youngest son, was Greig and Keith's constant companion. One day the barrio children presented ours with a pair of newborn twin goats, which became dearly loved pets. Then came a friendly monkey named Obal, which we later learned was the Maranao word for "monkey." Obal had to have a companion, of course, and we were never without pet monkeys from that moment on.

Since there was no market in Tugaya and meat was hard to come by, eggs were our chief source of protein. When we made our weekly mail run to Marawi City, we always brought back a hundred eggs, which we kept in a large bowl in the kitchen. Whenever Obal got loose from his bamboo pole outside the kitchen door, as sometimes happened, he would make a beeline for those eggs, picking them up dramatically one by one, and with a smirk on his face, he would smash them hard on the floor amidst our screams of, "Catch him, catch him!" Being a true monkey, he reveled in the attention.

Life in Tugaya Takes on a Routine

Each morning we were awakened at four o'clock by the call to prayer, when ceremonial ablutions are followed by supplications to Allah, with arms uplifted and faces turned toward Mecca. This ritual was repeated five times a day. In the midst of it all, Bob and I begged and borrowed every book we could lay our hands on which dealt with the subject of Islam and read voraciously.

Philippine maps indicated the cowpath to Tugaya as a national highway. Although this was the long-term vision of the central government, it was not more than wishful thinking when we arrived. The lake provided the only route for travel in those early years before jeepneys penetrated the mountain forest.

Once a week we would awaken the children at three o'clock and stumble for ten minutes in the pitch dark down to the lake in time to find seats on the launch. It was a breezy two hours by pump boat to the nearest market and post office, which were in Marawi City at the head of the lake. Marawi, known for its absence of cleanliness, boasted few streets back then and even fewer shops, so it was not hard to collect our few market and grocery items in time to catch the last launch back to Tugaya. The return trip was much more scenic, as we passed houses and mosques around the densely populated lakeshore. The launch left Marawi at noon in order to reach Tugaya ahead of the treacherous winds that swept across the lake every afternoon.

Wednesday mornings punctuated our week by half-days of prayer. With strict orders to lock the doors and let no one in, Bob and I would leave the three children in the care of our Visayan house girls. With a water bottle in one hand and Bible in the other, we would climb the steep ascent of a nearby hill. This secluded hilltop overlooking the lake offered the only place free from interruptions. Breathless, we would pause at the crest to drink in the serenity of the panorama below, which was as intensely beautiful as it was spiritually bleak. Metal-domed mosques glistened in the early morning sun. A thick vegetation of coconut and banana palms hid from view the people for whom we had come to intercede. Only the Holy Spirit could draw Muslim hearts to Himself, and each time we lifted our people to the Lord, our spirits were infused with new vision and a greater determination to keep going.

With a few medical supplies and basic medicines purchased from far-away Iligan City, we soon became known as the local clinic, especially since the nearest doctor of sorts was in inaccessible Marawi City. Whenever possible, I tried to limit this medical work to afternoons. One day a man came having slashed his arm with a knife. He was followed by another who had been kicked in the forehead by a horse, leaving a deep gash just above his eyebrow. Both men should have had stitches, but the nearest doctor was in Marawi City, two hours away by a launch that would not leave until the next morning. Without any medical training except for the brief first-aid course in jungle camp, we did what we could. In each case I gave a pain killer, cleansed the wound, and applied a butterfly bandage, trying my best to prevent it from leaving a scar.

It was my TB patients, however, who were the most interested in the gospel stories Bob was translating, which I read on my daily rounds. We were in radio communication with Linc Nelson, the missionary doctor near Nasuli, our Wycliffe base, and under his explicit directions, I was able to treat a number of chronic TB sufferers, all of whom were advanced cases. Sixty-five percent of the people had active TB, but without any diagnostic equipment, I could treat only the ones who were spitting blood. These were too far advanced to be permanently cured, but the injections added ten or fifteen years to the lives of most, long enough to raise their families. It was also long enough to hear the gospel and respond.

The local diet was lacking in protein, among other things, and there were no eggs for sale in Tugaya. Maranaos took a keen interest in our poultry project, which we started from white Leghorn layers, imported from a neighboring province. Eventually, one of the school teachers saw the potential for profit and followed our example, constructing a chicken coop like ours and importing layers from the coast, which was exactly what we had hoped would happen.

Shocking News

One morning a gentle knock on our door interrupted our peaceful routine.

"Your husband and son have been murdered!" was the devastating announcement.

Bob had left for town on his newly acquired motorcycle with five-year-old Greig riding behind him. They were on their way to Marawi City for a weekly mail and market run to spare the family the ordeal of getting up at 3:00 a.m. to catch the launch, since the lake was still the primary means of travel. A few minutes after Bob passed through one of the villages along the way, a man was murdered there. A notorious Muslim outlaw shot and killed a Visayan truck driver because he failed to stop and give him a ride. A woman in that village, however, had just seen Bob and Greig riding by and jumped to the conclusion that they were the victims. The "bamboo telegraph" sprang into action, and within a very short time the story had spread to Tugaya that the American and his son had been killed.

Finally, one of the young men mustered enough courage to climb the ladder and give me the tragic news. I then looked down from our porch to see a huge crowd of men and women—everyone from the barrio, it seemed—gathered in front of our house. They were shouting and most of them were armed with guns or carrying knives, determined to repay this Maranao who had murdered their American brother and his child.

Recovering from my initial shock, I went into the house as calmly as possible and told the frightened house girls that I needed to investigate an accident and would be back shortly. They were not Muslims—Maranao girls don't work for a living. These were Visayan girls from our base at Nasuli, and they were duly terrified. I instructed them to lock the door securely and look after the two younger children until I returned. I then accompanied the vast mob that was making its way up the hill toward the scene of the crime, a two-hour hike away.

Fortunately, several of our village leaders had the good sense to investigate the story as soon as the rumors reached them, and one of them had a bicycle. The excited crowd had climbed only a half-hour up the steep hill when the man on the bicycle returned with the joyful news that the Americans were not the victims! A couple of hours later Bob and Greig came sailing into the village unaware of what had happened, wondering what they had done to deserve such an enthusiastic reception. Crowds gathered around the motorcycle as it pulled to a stop in front of our house. They cheered and shouted their welcome and affectionately patted Greig on his arms and face, much to his consternation.

This was the first time we were keenly aware of angelic guardians in our volatile environment. But perhaps even more importantly, the outcome of this incident brought us closer to our barrio people, opening our hearts to them and theirs to us. It reinforced the loving relationship of those early years of language learning and linguistic analysis.

A Fiercely Proud People

Maranaos had asked us when we first arrived, "What is your purpose in coming here?"

"To learn your language," we told them truthfully.

Being somewhat arrogant, this seemed quite logical to them. As far as they were concerned, there were only two groups of people in the world who were of any significance, Maranaos and Americans, an opinion they had voiced more than once. Although they had retreated before the Spaniards, they were never subdued.

"The Spaniards never conquered us!" they boasted. "The Japanese never conquered us, and the Americans also did not conquer us! We are the ones who helped the Americans defeat the Japanese."

And indeed they had, at least in their mountain stronghold. Our landlord, Hadji Abdullah, had been a guerrilla fighter during World War II, helping the American troops to hold back the Japanese, who were never able to enter this province.

"After you learn our language, you will go back to America and teach everyone to speak Maranao!" they announced, not expecting any response in particular, and we gave none.

We simply smiled, careful not to mention that our ultimate goal was to translate the Bible into their language, and they were satisfied. Had we not been discreet, we would never have had the unprecedented opportunity of spending three years in the very heart of Maranao culture.

They would have driven us out before language learning ever got off the ground. This did happen later, but not until we had made the most of this favorable setting for language and acculturation and not until Bob had established an alphabet and made great strides in linguistic analysis.

Toward the end of our Tugaya sojourn, we were assigned to Manila, where I delivered Sharon, our youngest. The moment we returned with our newborn, the people affectionately dubbed her "Miss Tugaya." The title *Bubay sa Tugaya* literally means, "The Lady of Tugaya."

"Naturally, she is the Lady of Tugaya," the people informed us, "because she was conceived here."

Eventually our barrio people became aware that Bob was translating the Christian holy book. The local *imam* (Muslim priest) told Bob's language helper, Lawa, that he would go to hell if he continued to help, and he would most certainly go blind. He explained that not even one thousand pesos a day would atone for his sin of helping to translate the infidel's book. Finally, the once warm and cordial atmosphere turned hostile, even menacing, making it clear that we were no longer welcome in Tugaya.

The old sultan was dead by this time. Muslim hospitality had demanded that our landlord protect us from possible harm and danger. Hadji Abdullah had been a true friend, but now he was caught in an unenviable position and could no longer protect us. He urged us to leave but begged us not to transfer to another Muslim location for fear of losing face. He might be accused of betraying Muslim hospitality.

The following decade things progressed from bad to worse on the lake. By the mid-seventies Muslim fundamentalists began arriving from the Middle East to teach in the mosques. They taught our people that their enemy was the Jew and that the American was the friend of the Jew. Until then Maranaos had never even heard the word *Jew*. Terrorist organizations like Hamas and Hezbollah, sprang up in Marawi City.

We left Tugaya in 1964, not realizing we would never again be able to live on the lake, and it wasn't long before we couldn't even return to visit. Although Bob had made good headway in linguistics, he had been able to do very little actual Bible translation because of the unavailability of informants.

Chapter 3

A Door Opens in Wao

A Strange Invitation

Our Wycliffe director at Nasuli came to us one day with a letter from Wao (pronounced *wah-oh*), and attached to it was a long, impressive list of Arabic signatures. We had never even heard of Wao!

Driven out of Tugaya, with nowhere to continue our Maranao work, we had returned to Nasuli. Bob was asked to replace the base superintendent who was home on furlough, but at the end of the year's assignment, no door had opened for us. A term in those days was five years, and we had been there barely four. We were now seriously considering taking an early furlough when this letter arrived seemingly out of nowhere, with an invitation.

Wao is Maranao territory, and the people there wanted someone from Nasuli to live among them. Furthermore, to prove their sincerity, they had built an airstrip! Nevertheless, we were skeptical. Why would Muslims specifically request the presence of Christians in their community? We weren't about to sink roots down a second time in a Maranao village only to be driven out again, or worse. Was this a ruse? We couldn't leave for furlough, however, without checking it out.

Entrusting our children to the care of kind friends at the base, we flew twenty minutes over the mountains to the fertile farmlands of central Mindanao and landed in the barrio of Wao, where the cornfield had been converted into a grass landing strip. With no radio contact, we asked our pilot to pick us up in three days, dead or alive. During the days that followed we accepted Maranao hospitality, sleeping on their beds, drinking warm Cokes in the absence of clean water, talking with as many people as we could, and shocking everyone by communicating in their dialect.

Datu Tao was the headman in this "airport" barrio. He was an extremely influential figure for many hectares around, more powerful even than the sultan in town. If we did settle there, we needed to make a number of things crystal clear.

"We are Christian missionaries," we told him, using the strongest terms possible, to which he nodded his smiling head.

"Our purpose in coming is to translate the Christian Bible into your language," we continued, again with the same response. "And we will always need Maranaos to assist us in this work."

Datu Tao assured us that help would always be available and all our demands would be met, which left us more puzzled than ever. Why would Muslims respond like this?

Finally on the third day, the pieces of the puzzle began to fall into place and the enigma was solved. Because of vast tracts of undeveloped, fertile farmland, the central government had opened the entire area for resettlement, offering easy terms for land and tractors to lure the poor from overcrowded areas throughout the Philippines. Maranaos deeply resented this occupation of what they considered to be their turf, since they were the original inhabitants. Even though they could not possibly use all this land, they were ready to defend it with their lives, and blood flowed freely as Muslims and "Christians" battled for possession. The only medical help available for the wounded, however, was a government doctor in town who had very few supplies and no equipment whatsoever.

Datu Tao was concerned for his wounded and was searching for a way to get medical help for them. With no public transportation and only impassable roads, he turned his attention toward air travel. The nearest plane was at Nasuli, and he had heard that the presence of personnel from there would insure radio contact with the pilot and thus help for his injured. We were now holding the trump card! Maranaos needed us. Datu Tao readily gave his word that everything we requested would be provided, and he was as good as his word until the day he died many years later. Before we left Wao that third day, we agreed to come and live there.

The Poor Country Cousins

The majority of the people in the town of Wao were settlers from every island, representing nearly all the dialects of the Philippines. Datu Tao's barrio, however, was pure Maranao. It was a thirty-minute hike from town through the cornfields and across a river. Wao is actually in the same province as Marawi City, but it's over the mountains from the lake, with no roads linking the two. The only way to reach it was around the coast through three other provinces and back up to the inland mountain range. These Wao Muslims were the "poor country cousins," living far away from the center of Maranao culture and not as fanatical in the tenets of Islam. They were less sophisticated and had less exposure to Islamic teachings.

Bob went ahead of the family to oversee construction on a small bamboo house. This time it was easy to get labor from the settlers in town, who hailed from every island of the Philippines. There were twelve houses out in the barrio, and ours would make the thirteenth, the one nearest the airstrip. A Maranao had erected a bamboo framework for a house in that very spot but abandoned it because the site was haunted. Wanting to follow the local architecture, we simply bought this framework, which was a bargain since none of the locals were inclined to share a house with the spirits. We would deal with those demons later.

A Gala Reception

The people wanted to know when the family would be arriving so they could prepare a reception party for us. It had to be in the morning so that Bill Foster, the pilot, could stay for the festivities. Bill was a major figure in these proceedings, and had already won the hearts of the people with his friendly, outgoing personality. Finally, Bob set the date, and an excited family arrived for the historic occasion. Bill brought his lovely wife, Jane, with their two children on a second flight, making it an extra gala affair. The entire barrio gathered around, bearing quantities of sweet Muslim delicacies made from sticky rice and coconut milk, while teenage girls provided the entertainment with songs and dances. The fan dance was the main attraction, followed by the lyrics of traditional Muslim folklore, the singing of which mimics the chanting of the mosque. It was a warm reception indeed.

Settling into a Routine

Once more we settled into a Muslim barrio, but this time space was of the essence. These were not the wealthy smugglers who lived in big houses around the lake. They were poor farmers who lived in bamboo houses and ate only two meals a day. Built up on stilts, Wao houses were small, and with four children, our schoolroom took up most of the space. Little postage stamp bedrooms, a dining room, and kitchen circled the schoolroom, which opened out on an ample back porch framed by majestic, cyanic mountains in the background. This was our living room, while the front porch served as visiting area, with a bench built into its railing. Bob piped water into the kitchen from a rainwater tank on the roof and added the sophistication of an indoor outhouse by placing the "bathroom" on the back porch. An empty five-gallon kerosene can with a showerhead welded to the bottom provided the luxury of not only cold showers, but also hot ones when warmed with a kettle of boiling water. Evenings were chilly in the mountains. We were snug and ready to tackle school.

Several evenings a week we showed filmstrips, powered by a tiny generator, and these became a popular diversion, as the entire village gathered under our house. Old Testament stories were a big hit. Although Muhammad claimed that the

Koran was the result of a revelation from the angel Gabriel, his knowledge of the Bible came, in fact, from traveling Hebrew Christians, and these facts he altered to suit himself. Whenever the Koran disagreed with the Bible, like the substitution of Ishmael in place of Isaac as the son of promise, the people amiably overlooked our discrepancies for the sake of entertainment.

There are only two seasons in the tropics: the wet and the dry. When the rains come, temperatures cool to more comfortable levels. Being near the equator, Philippine seasons do not lengthen or shorten the days. Dusk falls at six o'clock all year round, signaling the lighting of cooking fires. By seven o'clock the rice is ready, and the family gathers outside to eat around the glowing embers. Evenings were short in Wao, except when we were showing filmstrips. With full tummies and no electricity, people retired early, lulled to sleep by breezes whispering through the cornfields and crickets performing their evening symphony. We soon learned to fit into this schedule, which provides a welcome head start to the following day.

Sunday Tradition

Filipino breakfasts typically feature dried fish, for which neither Bob nor I have ever acquired a taste. Our children, however, considered it a great delicacy, along with the usual rice. On Sunday mornings, therefore, after our family Sunday school, they feasted with our housegirl, after which she accompanied them for a swim in the shallow waterfalls while Bob and I took communion together. We had decided from the beginning on this type of Sunday observance, and in Wao as well as in Tugaya our people always respected Sunday as our holy day.

Strange Noises in the Night

Shortly after settling into our Wao routine, we were awakened one night by the sound of a stray animal under the house. It sounded like a carabao had been tied to a tree out in the fields but had broken loose and was rubbing its horns against the floorboards of the house. It was a familiar sound, not disturbing during the day, but in the middle of the night it was enough to keep us awake. When Bob went down with his flashlight to chase the carabao away, however, there was not an animal in sight. We went back to sleep only to have the same thing repeated. This time the whole house was swaying slightly. Again Bob went down, and again there was no animal in sight, either under the house or out in the cornfield. Just as we were dropping off to sleep for the third time, too weary to figure out what was happening, we were awakened once more! Finally the Holy Spirit got through to us that this was not a carabao but a demon. We dealt with the evil spirit swiftly, exorcising it. From this experience we learned the importance of spiritual cleansing of a house before moving into it. There were more haunted houses to come.

The Ladies' Social Hour

At last we were ready to launch a literacy program in Wao. The only person in the barrio who knew how to read was Makapantar, but even he was literate only in the Arabic script, which he had learned in the *madrasa* school at the mosque. As every good Muslim knows, Arabic is the language of heaven, and therefore it's a good idea to have a working knowledge of the language. After all, who wants to be a wallflower in heaven? Consequently, Maranao children attend *madrasas* on Friday and Saturday, where they are taught to read the Arabic letters. Oddly enough, however, no emphasis is placed on understanding, and Maranaos seldom know the meaning of a single word they are reading in Arabic. The only thing that matters is being able to read the Arabic letters with ease. This is due to the fact that Koranic reading contests are held annually throughout the Muslim world, and the winner is the one who can read from the Arabic Koran with the greatest fluency, with or without understanding.

Wao needed readers if our translation of the Bible was to benefit them, and so I issued the invitation. My literacy class was made up entirely of women, with the exception of Makapantar. Although he already knew how to sound out Maranao words written with Arabic letters, he decided he wanted to learn the Roman letters, too. Muslim women would normally be intimidated by the presence of a man, but the ladies soon learned to ignore Makapantar, who stayed unobtrusively in his corner. Every afternoon about eight women brought their babies and sat on the front porch facing a large blackboard that we hung outside the kitchen.

I used the phonics approach to literacy, which I was also using successfully with our own children. When each woman's turn came to sound out a letter or syllable, she would hand her baby to the woman next to her, who would obligingly continue nursing the infant at the other breast, along with her own. Cigarettes were also shared, and everyone got a puff as they were passed around. It was a congenial atmosphere, and my students learned quickly while enjoying the daily social hour.

During class Bob would sit inside, where he could hear what was going on without being seen. After the ladies left each afternoon, we would put our heads together to decide on the best pictures to draw in order to teach each letter and syllable. Together we prepared a large primer featuring Bob's artwork, which reflected his engineering background. When the Gospel of Mark was ready, the women were also ready to read it. That was a thrilling day for all of us, as Mark became our advanced "primer."

My dream had been to have Bible studies inside the mosque, and so we took our new primer into the mosque for our lesson. The arrangement didn't last long, however. The women were quite happy with it, but the *ustad*, the Islamic teacher who had been sent from the Lake, was not. Because they had heard that we were now living in Wao, the religious leaders in Marawi City had commissioned this young *ustad* to better indoctrinate their Wao "cousins" in the religion of Islam. He shouted his reprimand at the women, who made a meek and speedy retreat from the mosque. We did learn later that some of the men were slightly literate, and what a joy it was to see husband and wife pouring over the Gospel of Mark together.

A somewhat amusing yet sad epilogue to our literacy saga is how these primers were disposed of in the Lake area. The printing was done in Manila and funded by an educational organization in the States. Five thousand of these primers arrived in Lanao right in the middle of an election season. The entire country was caught up in the frenzy of campaigning, a time when candidates buy votes by handing out pesos to voters, who then respond with true Filipino loyalty on election day. One enterprising Maranao politician in Marawi City seized upon these large, attractive red books and used the entire supply of primers as campaign bribes, thus saving himself a huge amount of money! But alas, when missionaries in later years wanted to use them, there was not a primer to be found!

Electrifying Wao

During one of our furloughs, a Sunday school class in Seattle raised money for a small 1,500-watt generator for our family. We decided, however, that we couldn't enjoy electricity in the evenings without sharing it with our neighbors, so Bob offered to hook up lights for the other twelve houses if each household would purchase its own 20 Watt fluorescent bulb from town. Excitement ran high as each bulb was connected and every home lit up. The elders then came with much earnestness, imploring Bob to install a light in the mosque as well, which he did. It was not long, however, before our little generator puttered and sputtered and then expired. What we had not foreseen was that the people would add more bulbs of their own, without our knowledge, far exceeding the output capacity of our little generator. Electrifying Wao didn't last long, and we soon returned to our original eight o'clock bedtime along with the rest of the barrio.

Harmony

Saturday was the day for our family outings, either swimming at the waterfalls or hiking to town where the children could spend their pennies on local candy. They had seen an occasional horse riding through town and were begging for one of their own. Animals were an important part of their lives. They were often on the back of a nearby carabao, but there were no horses in our barrio. After our friends at Nasuli became aware that our children were praying earnestly for a horse, we received a radio message one morning from another translation team that a colt would soon be ready to leave its mother. Sadly, however, it was too far away to do us any good. Too far, that is, until Pilot Bill found out about it and offered to fly the young horse out to Wao. This was a daunting feat indeed in a small plane. The children quivered with excitement at the prospect and already had a name picked out for the young filly. Following the custom at Nasuli, the two single girls who were sending the horse had a team name, Harmony, which was derived from a combination of both of their last names. The children appropriately decided to name their horse Harmony after Aunt Pat and Aunt Shirley.

At last the big day arrived and Bill flew in the opposite direction from Wao to Harmony's barrio to pick up the horse, which had already been injected with a strong sedative in preparation for her journey. Since the starting point was farther away from us than Nasuli, the flight to Wao was much longer than usual, and before Bill had cleared the last mountain range, the plane began to tremble as Harmony started to wake up. Instantly, fervent prayers ascended for the plane's safety, both from our family as well as the girls. We were all glued to the radio, following every tremor of the flight. Loud cheers erupted as Bill buzzed our landing field while the people cleared it of animals and children. As we led the sleepy horse to her corral, the people of Wao stared in disbelief.

Linguistics

The process of entering a new language area and producing a translation of the Scriptures is somewhat complex. Along with learning the language is the analyzing of sounds and how they are produced, which is called phonetics. The next phase is phonemics, which is the study of how these sounds are used in different contexts. And the third part of linguistic analysis is morphology, or grammar, and includes the various affixes and suffixes that are added to the root form of a word to express differences in tense and mode, and so forth. These three aspects form the guidelines as to how the language is written so as to be most understandable to the native speaker. Wycliffe had trained us in all these areas of linguistics, which are also basic in deciding on an alphabet. Not all of our English letters are used in other languages. On the other hand, new sounds require new symbols or the new use of old ones. Bob got a good start on all of this while we were still in Tugaya, as well as taking his first baby steps in producing a translation of Mark, a popular Scripture to start with because it's the shortest gospel.

Back in Tugaya, our director had visited us a month after we first arrived in the Philippines and asked if I was doing any linguistics along with Bob. With three very small children, I laughed, and the director agreed.

"That's the way Jane and I feel," he said. "There's no point in two people changing diapers!"

Right from the start our roles were clearly defined, which proved the most efficient system in the long run. With added time at his desk, Bob gained more expertise in linguistics and translation than either of us could have if we were both translating as well as sharing domestic responsibilities.

The next step after linguistics is exegesis. Bob's seminary major in Greek and Hebrew prepared him well for this. It is basic to the first draft of the translation, and this is when language assistants, i.e. native speakers, play a major role in checking every word and phrase in the vernacular. Throughout the translation process the translator is dependent upon the Holy

Spirit for a perfect balance between being completely literal on the one hand, which results in a meaningless translation, and a very free expression on the other hand, which, though readily understood, is often far from the meaning the Holy Spirit intended.

Before publishing any of this translated material, two more steps are needed. One is to produce a back translation, translating the foreign language back into English to double check for accuracy, and the other is to publish a trial edition for testing with a number of native readers for readability and meaning.

Bible Translation

While we were still living in Tugaya, we heard about Victorio Dulog, a half-Maranao who lived in a distant province. Some years earlier he had been converted through missionaries who had sent him to their Bible school, where the only translation recognized as authentic was the King James Version of the Bible. Bob had hoped that Victorio, since he was a believer, would be his primary language assistant, but alas, Victorio could not be persuaded to simply check Bob's work with him. He insisted on a literal, word-for-word translation from the "inspired" King James Bible, thus producing a completely unintelligible version, which was tantamount to gibberish. Reluctantly, Bob turned elsewhere for language helpers.

As Datu Tao had promised, language assistants were always available in Wao. We were somewhat concerned, however, about dialect differences between Wao and the Lake. Although the few differences were slight and all the words were mutually intelligible in both areas, if Lakeside Maranaos picked up any vocabulary that was peculiar to Wao, they would look down on the translation as belonging to an inferior group of people. The Lake is the prestige area and home to more than 90 percent of Maranaos. If our translation was to be authentic, it needed to be pure for the people on the Lake and free from dialect corruption.

Bob's first language assistant in Wao was Macabanding. To our great relief, his dialect was unadulterated because he had been born and raised on the Lake. In his late teens, however, he had seduced one of his father's wives, which led to the pair's having to flee to escape the wrath at home. They ended up in Wao, raising their family and farming the land assigned them by Datu Tao. The Lord used even Macabanding's sordid past to further the work of Bible translation!

Ishmael was another long-time language assistant. Although he was a native of Wao, Bob was able to check over all of his work with Macabanding, as well as others from the Lake later. Several native speakers were always needed at this stage in translation.

Ishmael was also one of my chronic TB patients. Like most rural people, he would stop his TB treatment as soon as he felt better, before it was complete, and so the process had to be started all over again. This happened several times until, in later years, newer and more effective drugs became available and we were able to help him recover more or less permanently. Another chronic TB patient was Maludatu, who accompanied us to Nasuli for translation workshops on more than one occasion.

A Colporteur Trip

As soon as the Gospel of Mark was published, we were eager to get it into the hands of not only our Wao people, but also those around the Lake. So we launched a colporteur trip back to Lanao, starting at the Spencer plantation.

After the Spanish-American War, when the Philippines was ceded to America, the United States government sent a large group of educators to teach English in Filipino schools, and the Spencers were among those early arrivals. They were a Christian family who now owned a large coconut plantation in a Muslim province next to Lanao. We had often heard about the Spencers when we lived in Tugaya, and we were especially interested in meeting Mother Pearl, who, we learned, had had a vision at the time of her baptism in the Holy Spirit. In her vision she saw Maranaos worshiping Jesus at the foot of the cross and recognized them by the way the women were dressed. Various Filipino tribes wear the colorful circular garment called a *malong*, but Maranao women have their own style of drawing part of the *malong* up over the left shoulder and securing the rest above the bust, whereas the other Filipinos simply tie it around the waist. This Maranao fashion makes household chores more difficult, but it also expresses the pride with which Maranaos consider themselves superior to all other peoples and their women, above doing housework.

We needed Mother Pearl's inspiration before starting our trip around the Lake, which is why we flew from Nasuli to the Spencer plantation first. We spent two incredible days listening to Mother Pearl and her conviction that there would surely be a mighty harvest of Maranaos coming to Christ. And indeed there will be.

Returning to Tugaya, however, was disappointing. The cowpath had been widened to allow public jeepneys to make their way around the lake. We had sold a number of copies of Mark to Maranaos in jeepneys along the road and to a few to crowds who gathered in barrios, but we were not able to sell a single copy in Tugaya. In our absence, a number of *hadjis* had studied Islamics in Egypt and had since returned. The atmosphere was even more fanatically Muslim than when we lived there. The mosque, which the people started building back then, was now 40 feet high with ornate designs carved in concrete. It was built entirely by volunteer labor, with plans for it to go even higher. A generator lit up the mosque area at night, and a loudspeaker broadcasted the call to prayer five times a day.

As soon as we arrived in Tugaya, we reported to the new mayor, who gave us a cordial welcome and assigned us a place to stay, which turned out to be our old home. As we walked up past the mosque, a huge crowd gathered around to see what we were selling. The local *imam* (priest) soon recognized our books. Not realizing that we understood him, he warned the people to have nothing to do with us and instructed them to get as many of our books as they could and throw them down the toilet pits, adding obscenities. Then smiling broadly at us, he used very elementary Maranao and asked us to give our books to the eminent members of the crowd, gesturing elaborately! With some difficulty, we slipped away from the contemptuous mob.

Tugaya is a municipality that covers an unusually large area, much bigger than a barrio. Rising at dawn the next morning, we tramped to the farthest end trying to sell Mark. Everywhere we went the answer was the same: "We will go blind if we read that book," or "We will go to hell." We returned from our fruitless hike to have lunch with a former TB patient, Mauke. Realizing that we would never sell the Scriptures in Tugaya, we began giving them away secretly, in homes where we were reasonably sure they would not be burned or destroyed. We gave them to former TB patients, several schoolteachers, and to Lawa, Bob's old language helper, seven copies in all.

Public opinion was so strong in Tugaya and the religious leaders so hostile that even the people who had been cordial inside their homes turned the other way as they passed us on the trails. People standing in the doorways of their houses made a quick retreat when they saw us coming, not wanting to invite us in. We left after three days with the prayer that the seven people in Tugaya who now owned a copy of Mark would indeed read it and share it with others.

It was a comforting relief to return to Wao after the hostility on the lake.

Chapter 4

Encounter with the Holy Spirit

The Sherrill's Book

It was 1966, and our first furlough was due. We planned a short one, both for the sake of our children as well as for our work. A year in the States can be unsettling for young ones, who barely have a chance to adjust to a new school and make a few friends before they are yanked out and returned to the field.

A short furlough, however, can be hectic, especially when the couple hails from opposite shores of the continent. We divided our time between Seattle and the East Coast, which included New Jersey as well as Long Island, where we had spent the first four years of our marriage.

It was on Long Island, while attending an inter-denominational church that had started in our home, that we met an Episcopalian woman who had been involved in the Charismatic Renewal in California. I was sitting next to her at a church dinner one weekend when she shared with me what the Holy Spirit meant to her. As Valerie spoke, I didn't have a clue what she was talking about, but her effervescence and joy were attractive. I noticed also that she hadn't touched her food. She seemed to have other nourishment. One Sunday morning she brought me John and Elizabeth Sherrill's book *They Speak with Other Tongues*, which I returned unread a couple of weeks later.

"I'm sorry, Valerie," I apologized, "but I haven't had time to read this, and we're leaving for Seattle this week."

"Seattle!" she exclaimed. "That's where all this is going on!"

All what, I wondered. Valerie looked me in the eye. If I would promise to keep the book moving, I could keep it. I dutifully promised, and she pressed another one into my hand, a pamphlet by Derek Prince called *Baptism in the Holy Spirit.* She urged us to visit St. Luke's Episcopal Church when we got to Seattle.

I never read in the car. It always makes me carsick, and in 1966 my travel time was usually spent trying to keep four young children occupied and squabbles down to a minimum. When exhausted by that job, I would claim my turn at the wheel. This trip, however, was different from the start. As we pulled out of my parents' driveway in New Jersey, I picked up the Sherrils book, a well-told firsthand account of the charismatic awakening of the sixties, told in a dramatic style. I hardly stopped reading for three days while God kept my tummy calm and the children peacefully occupied.

It doesn't take much to convince a person working with Muslims that he needs the Holy Spirit's power. As I read, I kept exclaiming excitedly to Bob, "This is what we need." I knew we needed help in reaching Muslims for Christ. He was unimpressed, but I was too focused on the subject at hand to be concerned by his response, or lack of it. With his Dallas Seminary background, which teaches that the gifts of the Spirit ceased with the early church, this was forbidden territory, and his theological position was clearly defined. When we finally visited St. Luke's, his only purpose in going was to make sure his wife didn't go rolling down the aisles. The moment we arrived for the midweek service, however, he was drawn as if by a magnet to the atmosphere of praise. Throughout his seminary days he had longed to praise the Lord the way these gentle Episcopalians were doing. And so it was that Dennis Bennett, "the Father of the charismatic movement," as he is affectionately dubbed, laid hands on Bob to receive the Holy Spirit's baptism. We left Seattle after a month, both bubbling over with the joy of the Holy Spirit. As we boarded our ship back to the Philippines, we shared what God had done for us with several Christians on board. One by one, each of them came to our cabin asking for the laying-on of hands to receive the baptism with the Holy Spirit, an experience that changed each of their lives, as it had ours.

Realizing how controversial this subject was, however, we had agreed before leaving Seattle not to talk about it when we arrived back at Nasuli, our base. But this was the mid-sixties, the early days of the Charismatic Renewal. God was pouring out His Holy Spirit all over the world, and Nasuli was no exception. People were hungry for God, so much so that one-third of our missionaries came into this new relationship with the Holy Spirit. Bob and I simply happened to be on hand at that point in time.

God Heals in Wao

When we returned to Wao, we were immediately caught up in a display of God's power as Maranaos found themselves raised from deathbeds by prayer offered in the name of Jesus.

A messenger knocked on our door one afternoon requesting the plane to take a woman who was dying of TB to the nearby mission clinic. She was vomiting literally basins of blood, and the government doctor in town, after giving her what medications he had, said she would not last through the night. They arrived at our house, however, after the noon radio schedule with Nasuli, and there was no way to make contact with the pilot until 5:00 p.m., which was too late in the day for the plane to come and get back before dark.

Moved by the hopelessness of the situation, we did something we had never done before. We had never prayed for the sick, but it was the only thing we could do. We hiked across the fields and valley to the isolated farmhouse and knelt down by her mat. After laying hands on her forehead and offering prayer in the name of Jesus, we left her as we had found her, helpless in a dark corner of the hut, too weak to speak.

At daybreak the next morning, opening wooden windows,

I was shocked to see the same woman rise from the stretcher on which she had been carried and climb unassisted up the steep steps to our porch.

In response to my stunned expression, she said, "I spat only a tiny drop of blood last night," and she raised the tip of her pinky to show how little blood she had lost.

Then she added, "Your prayers healed me."

The plane came for the "dying" woman that morning and took her to the mission clinic, where she was treated for advanced-stage TB. But her healing had begun the night before in Wao. Against all odds, she was back working in the family rice fields before long and still was the last time we inquired about her, which was twenty years later!

That same week, Maranaos from a village that was two hours' hiking distance away arrived on our porch carrying a woman who needed immediate surgery. Her abdomen was so swollen that she looked like she was about to deliver a baby, but she wasn't pregnant. She had an obstruction, that had prevented her bladder from functioning for the past three days. The doctor in town had said she would be dead by morning if she didn't have surgery that very day. The town lacked electricity as well as most other requirements for surgery, not the least of which was a surgeon. The nearest help was the Baptist clinic near Nasuli.

Once again, the sad story was that after carrying their heavy burden a long distance under the broiling sun, the little party had arrived too late in the day for us to make radio contact with the pilot in time for him to come that afternoon. Sadly, they carried their patient up the long, steep ladder next door and laid the dying woman on the floor of the barrio captain's home. Maranaos want to be surrounded by as many people as possible when they die, and so the entire village crowded into the small bamboo house to help her die.

Once again moved by the utter hopelessness of the situation, we went next door wondering if our Muslim people would allow us to pray for the woman. Prayer was not the issue.

Muslims pray, five times a day in fact. Jesus was the issue. We couldn't pray for her without mentioning Jesus, but praying in His name was not only offensive, it was blasphemy.

We climbed the ladder and went quickly to the corner of the room where the dying woman lay on the floor, hoping we wouldn't be thrown out before we had a chance to pray. The wooden windows were all closed, shutting out light and filling the house with gloom.

With every eye strained on us, we turned to face the crowd and explained, "We are going to pray to Jesus and ask Him to heal her."

The thought crossed my mind, "And what if He doesn't?" Some of the faces took on a sinister expression. Not waiting for the permission that would never be granted, we turned quickly toward the patient to lay hands on her and prayed softly. No one in the room stirred as we slipped out as quickly as we had entered.

At dawn the next morning as I was opening our wooden windows before roll call on the radio, I noticed our next-door neighbor, the barrio captain, coming down the ladder from his house.

"Where is the sick woman?" I asked. "Does she still want the plane?"

"Oh, she walked home," he answered. Then noticing the shocked look on my face, he added, "Your prayers healed her."

Our faith was still smaller than a mustard seed. We had only enough faith to reach out and lay hands on a Muslim in the name of Jesus, but not enough to look for an answer. Yet that was enough for God. He did the rest, and we could hardly believe our eyes. People kept coming, and all were healed and we never got used to it.

Maranao houses, like most barrio homes in the Philippines, are built high off the ground to keep out snakes and torrential rains. Often the barrio people, however, don't get around to adding some of the finishing touches, like railings on porches to keep their toddlers from falling off. One day the inevitable happened. A two-year-old fell from the porch while his mother's back was turned, and he lay unconscious on the ground. The father came over frantically asking Bob to do what he could for his child, who had fallen from the porch. Actually, what was happening was a Muslim man was asking Bob to pray for his son, who was in critical condition, although he could not bring himself to articulate this request for prayer. Bob went with him, laid hands on the child, and prayed in the name of Jesus, loudly and clearly in the dialect so that all around would understand whom he was praying to. Later that afternoon we visited the family and learned that the little boy had gotten right up and had been playing peacefully ever since.

Besides illnesses that left in the name of Jesus, demons also left. A small girl had gone to the river alone one afternoon, which was not a good idea on two counts. As all animistic people believe, demons inhabit bodies of water. Furthermore, it's against their culture to go anywhere alone, ruled as they are by fear. Within minutes, the child was screaming in pain. She was doubled over with intermittent attacks in her abdomen, which continued for the rest of that day and night. The next morning they brought her to us, but told us nothing except that she had these attacks of pain.

When we asked how long she had been in pain and learned that it started when she went down to the river alone, we said, "Oh, this is a demon!"

"Yes," they agreed. "It is Satan."

Pagans are more in touch with the spirit world than most of us from the West. The people knew exactly what had happened. Muslims have a large share of animism mixed in with Islam, which is in fact folk Islam, practiced by rural people throughout the Muslim world. These animistic Muslims were keenly aware of evil spirits.

"This is easy," we told them. "Jesus is more powerful than Satan."

We took authority over the demon in the name of Jesus,

and the girl never had another attack. She stayed that afternoon to play happily under our house with Sharon, our youngest.

And so it went. Jesus was healing Maranaos. The climax, which is indelibly etched on our memory, came one Sunday. Our simple family worship concluded that morning, and I was making a Sunday morning brunch of French pancakes when Mina, the village *imam*, came and asked Bob to come to his house and pray for his brother-in-law, the barrio captain, who was dying of a virulent case of dysentery. The doctor in town had given him what medication he had and then sent him home to die. The barrio captain was our next-door neighbor, but the amoeba had struck so swiftly that we weren't even aware that he was sick. The *imam's* house was twice as large as his, so the relatives had carried the barrio captain there to make it possible for more people to crowd in and help him die. The entire village was on hand, in fact.

Bob took with him his newly translated Gospel of Mark and explained to the crowd, "I'm going to read some stories about sick people and how Jesus healed them."

There were no more dark looks. He did not have to wonder whether anyone would throw him out. Instead, there was expectancy on every face.

"Jesus healed many sick people when He was here on earth," Bob continued, "and He is still alive today."

So far so good. The Koran teaches that Jesus healed while he was here on Earth. Muslims also believe that Jesus is still alive because he never died. He was such a good man that it was unthinkable that Allah would allow him to die on a cruel cross. Instead, Allah rescued him in the nick of time and substituted Judas in his place, taking Jesus alive to paradise. Like Enoch, Jesus was translated without having died. Thus the cross, the heart of the gospel message, is neatly removed from the teachings of Islam, Satan's most powerful counterfeit.

Bob continued, "Jesus is still performing these miracles and healing people today." This was a departure from the faith. Nevertheless, God had already demonstrated this truth in their midst, and they were willing to listen while Bob preached the gospel that day and read to them about the healing of the blind man and the paralyzed man and the leper. Then he knelt down by the emaciated body lying on the floor beside him and laid hands on the barrio captain's head, praying in the powerful name of Jesus. He prayed in Maranao, clearly and distinctly so that everyone could hear and understand.

As usual, next morning just before radio roll call, I was lifting the wooden windows and securing each prop in place, when out of the corner of one eye I was startled to see a man coming down the ladder next door. I thought, surely it couldn't be the barrio captain since he was over at the *imam's* house. But it was!

"What are you doing up?" I asked, recovering myself. "I thought you were over at Mina's house."

Again the familiar answer came in the dialect, "Oh, your prayers healed me."

We were seeing Jesus heal in Wao, but it was happening so fast that it always took us off guard. It certainly wasn't our faith. We had so little. God was sovereignly revealing Himself through signs and wonders to Muslims. Our hopes soared. We were expecting a "peoples' movement," the whole village turning to Christ en masse. We pictured the baptismal scene at the river! We could see the village mosque being turned into a place of worship where the triune God was exalted, Jesus was given His rightful place as God's beloved Son, and the Holy Spirit was recognized personally as the third member of the Godhead.

One day we had a chance to voice the burning question in our hearts: What will you do with Jesus?

It was in the midst of wedding festivities, when no work was going on in the barrio that day. The village elders were sitting on a log in the clearing, and we joined them.

"You have seen Jesus heal your people when they were dying," we said to them. "Now what will you do with Jesus, God's Son?"

Never will we forget the answer that came from those

Muslim lips that day, "Oh, that wasn't Jesus! That was you!"

A sledgehammer could not have struck a more sickening blow. We couldn't believe our ears. We had been so careful each time we prayed to make sure they understood we were praying in the name of Jesus and that all that was accomplished in their midst was the result of the power of God in answer to prayer offered in the mighty name of Jesus. And we had assured them many times that we ourselves had absolutely no power.

Just as you never win a Muslim to Christ by argument, neither do you ever win an argument with a Muslim! We had learned that early on. Muslims love to debate, and they will go round and round in circles, never conceding defeat. They never lose.

"If you had not been here," they parried, "our sick people would not have been healed."

"That's true," we agreed. "If we had not been here, there would have been no one to pray to God for them. But we did not do the healing. We can't. We have no power. It was God's power, in answer to prayer offered in Jesus' name, which healed your sick people."

And so the argument went, round and round, and at the end of an hour we were back where we started. We felt sick in the pit of our stomachs.

Yes, Jesus was more powerful than Muhammad, they agreed, yet no one was willing to believe He was God's Son. The Koran clearly teaches that any follower of Islam who turns away from the faith is worthy of death, and this is not dead theology. When the people in Marawi City heard that we had settled in Wao, they did not dare harm us because we were under the protection of Datu Tao, the most powerful ruler for many kilometers around. Instead, they sent *ustads* and *tabligs* (Muslim teachers) to indoctrinate our barrio people more clearly in the tenets of Islam, and they did their work well while we lived there in the sixties and seventies.

We rose to leave that afternoon, walking sadly back to our house. That was probably the darkest hour of our Philippine sojourn. We had hit rock bottom. Tempted though we were to pack up and leave, the Lord reminded us, "I gave you a job to do, and it's not finished."

The healings stopped as suddenly as they had begun.

Chapter 5

The Fire Spreads

While three of our children were studying at the Nasuli school for the month before conference, we were out in Wao with only Sharon, our youngest. Bob needed to stay out a couple more weeks to finish what he was working on, so Sharon and I preceded him back to the base in order to have more time with our other children.

It was always a joyful reunion after our family had been separated, and friends from the dorm crowded into our house along with our children to welcome us back. All of them were excited when parents returned to the base, even if it was someone else's parents. The seventh and eighth grade was made up almost entirely of boys that year, and these were Greig's classmates from OCHO, an acronym for Older Children's Home. They were back after supper, too, joining in our evening devotions. I was reading from the Narnia books, an all-time favorite.

A Request

A couple of days after I arrived, a letter came from the Mayfields, who were translators furloughing in Seattle. They had served as house parents the year before they left and were very popular with the kids. I had been too busy that day to read the letter, but it occurred to me when the boys came that evening that they might like to hear the letter too, since the younger Mayfield children had been their good friends.

"Would you kids like to hear this letter from the Mayfields?" I asked.

"Oh yes," they chorused enthusiastically.

I began reading the letter, when suddenly I came to the segment describing the Mayfields' involvement at St. Luke's Episcopal Church in Seattle, the same place where we had been introduced to the Charismatic Renewal two years earlier. I paused, wishing I had not started this letter. If I stopped at that point, however, the boys would be consumed with curiosity and it would be worse than not finishing. I proceeded, hoping that the controversial subject matter would pass over their heads.

Eight o'clock came, and it was time for evening study hall at the school library. I had noticed Peter, who was one of the seventh graders, writing while I was reading and thought he was probably getting a head start on his homework. As the boys filed out, Peter dropped a slip of paper in my lap, which I didn't have a chance to look at until I had tucked our younger children in bed. When I finally read it, I was dumbfounded.

"Dear Aunt Mariel," Peter had scribbled. "I'm glad the Lord brought me here tonight. I need what the Mayfields got. In fact, all of Nasuli needs what the Mayfields got. Can you help me?"

I wasn't sure I could help Peter, but that wasn't the point. This was not a subject I wanted to get into, as not all the parents were sympathetic. As I left the *sala* to go downstairs to my study, wondering how on earth I was going to answer Peter, I shot up an SOS to heaven.

"Lord, what should I tell him?"

God's answer came in the form of two questions. Our old neighborhood in Stony Brook flashed before my mind, with the focus on one family in particular who were atheists.

"Would you lead their children to a saving faith in Me if you had the chance?" was the first question.

"Oh, yes, Lord!" I answered without hesitation, "even if the parents were angry and never spoke to me again."

"Then how important is this experience?"

I replied instantly, "It's the difference between a mediocre and a power-filled Christian life." That settled it for me.

The next evening, the kids were back. When the Narnia chapter ended and it was time for study hall, Peter and another boy paused on their way out, with questioning looks.

"The first thing you need to do is read the Book of Acts, chapters 1–11 and 19," I said, answering their unspoken query.

This will keep them busy for a week, I thought, grateful for the delay. The next evening was Wednesday, and I continued with Narnia as though nothing else mattered. As they filed out for study hall, however, there were now several boys waiting at the door with Peter.

"We finished those chapters in Acts," Peter spoke for all of them.

I was taken back by how quickly they had read them. What should I tell them next? I wondered. Unable to think of anything else, I handed them a book, *They Speak with Other Tongues*, by John Sherrill. In 1968 that was practically the only thing in print on the subject. I was sure it would take them at least a week to plow through it, but I was wrong again. They returned on Thursday evening with the same report.

"We finished the book!"

I was astounded. How was it possible for all of these seventh and eighth-grade boys to finish the book in twenty-four hours? I learned later from their teacher that they had taken turns reading to each other. During school recess, instead of climbing trees they gathered under the shade of a mango tree while one boy read to the rest. After recess, however, when their teacher asked them to put the book away, they were quick to obey. They kept up this reading aloud to each other during every free moment for the rest of that day, opting even to forgo their afternoon swim in the cool, spring-fed swimming hole in favor of finishing the book.

Only God could put such hunger for His Spirit in the hearts of boys this age. C. S. Lewis now paled in comparison, and Narnia would have to wait for another day. There was only one other thing I could think of doing and that was to play a record for them. It was a long-playing record with three men giving their testimonies about the Holy Spirit, extremely boring for these boys, I thought. Instead, they listened with such rapt attention you would think they were watching a live baseball game.

"We're comin' back tomorrow night to get it!" Peter warned as the record ended.

Tomorrow night being Friday, there would be no study hall, and the kids were free to do as they pleased for the entire evening. In the meantime, I bumped into the base director Friday afternoon.

"I understand the children are coming to your house tomorrow evening to speak in tongues," he said with a questioning look.

I had no answer, and he continued, "I'm going to ask them not to come."

"Dick," I said with a boldness that surprised me, "you can stop the boys from coming to our house, but you can't stop the Holy Spirit!"

Dick was taken back by the thought that he might be opposing the Holy Spirit.

"Come to my office later and we'll talk," he said.

When I arrived for our appointment, I handed Dick the note from Peter, and it was his turn to be surprised. He had assumed the whole thing was my idea.

As we chatted, he said three different times, "I'm not going to stop them." Then he added, "I have one request, however. Please do not teach the boys to speak in tongues."

I laughed heartily. This was a rumor I had not heard about. I promised solemnly not to teach anyone to speak in tongues.

The Gentle Wind of the Holy Spirit

After supper that evening, as I waited for the boys to arrive, I was filled with apprehension. Bob and I had always prayed together for people to receive the baptism. Now I was alone and feeling very inadequate.

"Did you think *you* had anything to give the boys?" the

Lord asked by way of gentle rebuke. And then I realized, of course not! I had nothing to offer them. The Lord was the one who had placed this hunger in their hearts in the first place, and He was the only one who could satisfy it.

The boys arrived exploding with excitement as they filled the rattan chairs in the *sala*. Later I learned that they had all fasted supper that evening in their eagerness to receive all that God had for them. This, understandably, upset the house parents, who were new that year and felt responsible for both the mental and physical health of the children under their care.

The Lord had already impressed on me that I should emphasize holiness in talking to the kids. "We're not going to talk about speaking in tongues," I began to everyone's disappointment. The expression on their faces said, What do you think we're here for?

"We must have clean hearts if we want the Holy Spirit to fill us," I continued. "We need to start by asking God to search our hearts and confessing whatever sins are there, because sin will block God's blessing in our lives."

They immediately started praying, going around the room one by one. Their prayers were general but offered with such earnestness that one would think they had been hardened criminals. As the prayers concluded, I looked to the Lord for the next step.

"Now, I'll lay hands on each of your heads and pray for you." After doing that I sat down, wondering again what to do next. I thought back to St. Luke's.

"Lift your arms to God and just start praising Him," I instructed. That's what they did at St. Luke's, I remembered.

Raising hands in worship was Scriptural, I knew. It was a sign of surrender to God as well as praise.

As they did this, I noticed Peter's older brother, Danny, on the rattan sofa. He looked like he was leaning to one side, almost as though he might fall over. I was terrified by the possibility that this might be a demonic manifestation. I had never heard of being slain in the Spirit. I had no idea what a beautiful experience it was and that it was often accompanied by visions and visitations from God. My fear of the demonic was so great that I pled with God not to let Danny fall over. He didn't. The Lord took pity on my ignorance, which robbed this eighth-grade boy of what may possibly have been one of the most significant experiences of his life.

Almost immediately, however, Danny began speaking softly in a beautiful, unknown language as I sighed in relief. This was followed by what sounded like the ripple of a babbling brook as each boy, one by one around the room, began gently praying in tongues. The sound was harmonious, like a mellow symphony.

After a few minutes of praising God in tongues, it dawned on the boys what had happened. They all jumped to their feet in excitement, and Peter exclaimed, "We've got to go all over the base and tell everyone about this." Oh, no, I thought. I panicked!

"Go and tell Aunt Nadine," I urged them, trying to channel their energy.

With that they all made a dash out the front door and across the base to Nadine's house. I knew she would be pleased, and she did indeed encourage them in their new encounter with the Holy Spirit. When the boys returned, it was almost time for the generator to be turned off. The whole base would soon be plunged into darkness, and they charged back to OCHO before the lights went out.

The boys returned every evening after that, no longer to listen to the reading of Narnia, but to pray for others who wanted Jesus to baptize them in the Holy Spirit. The fifth and sixth graders were now coming, and we would all gather around to lay hands on each one while the Lord poured out His Spirit. This was revival. No one but God Himself could have put the intensity of spiritual hunger in the hearts of boys that age, or in anyone, for that matter.

A week went by, and the following Sunday morning after church Dick said to me, "We're going to ask the children not to go to your house any more."

I knew this would happen eventually, and I didn't blame Dick, as director, for taking this action. I nodded in agreement.

Sunday Afternoon

Rest hour was strictly observed on Sunday afternoons, and the base was quiet until three o'clock. On the dot of 3 p.m. that Sunday I heard my name being called from outside: "Aunt Mariel!" I went to the door, and there was every one of the OCHO kids, looking at me accusingly.

"We're not allowed to come to your house any more," they said with a tinge of anger in their voices.

"I know," I nodded.

"They said you agreed!" they added reproachfully.

"What was I supposed to do?" I asked.

"But Kathy wants the baptism!"

My heart leapt within me. Kathy was an eighth grader who had been teased mercilessly, even cruelly, as only children can do to each other. That is, until the Holy Spirit had taken hold of the boys, and their behavior toward her had changed dramatically. They were now treating her like a queen, and Kathy found this transformation irresistible. I had wept over Kathy's pain, but now her healing had begun as the Lord poured His love into her through her radically changed classmates.

"You know what to do," I challenged the kids.

A light went on in Peter's head and he yelled, "The fort!"

With one great surge, the kids tore off toward some secret place of their own at the other end of the base. Kathy wrote me a letter the next day telling about her beautiful experience that afternoon. This was also when our Carole, along with the other fifth and sixth graders, was baptized in the Holy Spirit, an experience that has influenced her entire life.

I had already counseled the boys about the importance of keeping a quiet time each morning and not neglecting the gift the Lord had given them. That Sunday evening at OCHO the director, along with several adults, mindful of the verse, "Forbid not to speak with tongues" I Corinthians 14:39), instructed the kids on the use of this gift. They were asked never to speak in tongues when they were together as a group. Their prayer language, they were told, was only to be used privately, when they were alone.

Very obediently, before breakfast every morning, a number of the boys would go out to the airfield and split up so they could pray aloud in tongues, separately, as part of their worship to the Lord. This way they would not be guilty of disobeying their elders.

The revival didn't end as joyfully as it had begun, however. Parents arrived at Nasuli for our biennial branch conference, understandably upset. Coming from a variety of denominational backgrounds, not all the missionaries were able to accept the Charismatic Renewal. This was the sixties, however, and God was pouring out His Spirit all over the world. No country or continent was excluded. But while some were hungry for God, not all were sympathetic. The experience doesn't fit neatly into everyone's theology.

Chapter 6

The Blackshirt/Ilaga War

A Bloody War Between Muslims and "Christians"

We had a number of years of fruitful translation work in Wao before the Blackshirt/Ilaga War broke out in the early seventies. By the time Bob finished three Gospels and several short Epistles, the conflict began. Muslims were always at war with their "Christian" neighbors over land disputes, but this conflict was more violent than others. The Blackshirts hailed from Cotabato, a neighboring Muslim province that was home to the Maguindanao, but the war soon spread to our province of Lanao del Sur. All Muslims, regardless of dialect, were automatically in the Blackshirt camp.

Ilagas were Visayans, which is the largest ethnic group in the Philippines and includes the many Visayan islands as well as our large island of Mindanao. Like most Filipinos, Ilagas practiced a form of Catholicism deeply rooted in animism. Ilaga warriors were steeped in the occult and boasted divine protection from their shaman practices. Satan is powerful and, indeed, many of them did display supernatural powers. They rubbed a specially "blessed" oil on their chest that actually rendered some of them invincible, or so they claimed.

Before we were even aware of this war, however, the Lord nudged us to move our family away from Wao to the coastal city of Iligan. Although Iligan is actually nearer to Lake Lanao than Wao is, it is nevertheless in a separate province and heavily guarded against Muslim aggression. We were safer there.

We were not yet settled in Iligan when news reached us

of an Ilaga attack upon our village in Wao. Our people from all twelve houses huddled in the mosque for protection, which made them easy targets. The Ilagas threw a bomb into the mosque, killing two people, one of whom was Datu Tao's second wife, Taraga, my closest friend in Wao. The Muslims retaliated by killing six Ilagas and then fled in a mass exodus from the area. If we had stayed, we would have been exceedingly vulnerable, caught between two warring forces. Our omniscient heavenly Father had moved us out in time.

The only road out of Wao was unsafe for Muslims, so our barrio people did the only thing they could. They followed a narrow footpath over the mountains to Marawi City at the head of the lake. It is possible for able-bodied young men to cross this mountain range in two days, but for this motley group of families with small children it took more than three days through bandit-infested jungle. The only food they had on the entire trip was a few berries and plants they foraged along the way. It was a dangerous route even for Muslims because of the outlaws hiding out in the dense woods. When they arrived in Marawi City, two children were missing, lost forever in the forest!

A Dearth of Language Assistants

In the meantime, Bob was searching for language assistants, whom we thought would be readily available in Iligan. It borders Maranao territory, yet it is far enough away for a Maranao working with us to be safe from the scrutiny of the *imams* on the Lake, or so we thought. But the road to finding one was not as easy as we had hoped. Two men from Marawi proved unfruitful, cunningly altering words and sentence structure to agree with Islam. Bob spotted the corruption immediately and was forced to let them go. This was a discouraging development.

One day someone referred Bob to Hadji Omar Ali from Marawi City, who agreed to work if the price was right. High salaries had always been a factor in working with Muslims, so Bob was prepared to pay whatever it took and readily agreed to the exorbitant amount Omar Ali demanded. Finally Ali was satisfied.

"After all, I do not have to believe what I do not agree with," he said, smiling as they closed the deal.

The next afternoon Bob went to his office in town with keen anticipation, eager to begin work with his new language assistant. Instead of Omar Ali knocking on his door at 1:30 that afternoon, however, a messenger appeared several hours later with Omar's formal and courteous letter explaining why, on second thought, he could not help with the translation of the Bible.

"For realizing the advantages and disadvantages worldly and heavenly," Ali wrote, "and with the advice of my relatives and the high hierarchy of the Muslim faith, I definitely decline the offer."

Bob was crushed. It had seemed like such a wonderful answer to prayer. Hadji Omar was better educated and more sophisticated than any language helper he had ever worked with, a suitable change at this stage in translation work. A trip to the local mosque, however, ended for Omar Ali in the all-too-familiar verdict. After ten years of living amongst Maranaos, we had the dubious distinction of being engaged in work that is "dangerous to the salvation of the faithful." Apparently there was not an *imam* in the entire area who was not familiar with our purpose for being there, and they all knew the evils of Bible translation and its potential threat to Islam in the Philippines.

God's Solution

Our faithful God, who makes all things work together for good, came to the rescue once again with a surprising solution. Shortly after this last disappointment, our Wycliffe director happened to be visiting us. As we were giving him a guided tour of nearby Marawi City, who should we run into but Maludatu, one of our friends from Wao. He jumped into our SUV and directed us to the section of the city where most of the families from our former barrio were crammed into two city houses! This is when we learned of the Ilaga attack on Wao and the tragedy of the bomb thrown into the mosque, followed by the Maranaos's eventful and hair-raising escape over the mountains. They had arrived in Marawi only a few days earlier with nothing but the clothes on their backs. They were surrounded by their well-fed Muslim brothers, who ignored their desperate need for food and clothing.

Somewhat dazed, we found ourselves plunging into a relief program that gained momentum over the following months. Generous gifts poured in from our fellow missionaries at Nasuli, which enabled us to deliver rice, dried fish, and clothing to our forlorn friends on a regular basis for several months to come, until they were able to return to Wao.

While I scheduled these weekly deliveries to Marawi City in the afternoons after school was over, Bob made full use of the Wao refugees, who were now only an hour away from us by public transportation. He had all his old language assistants nearby and all the help he could use, which was nothing short of miraculous. God had indeed come through for us yet again. The Epistles of James and John had just come off the press, and I was distributing them along with relief supplies. What could be a more appropriate backdrop for a practical Epistle like James than the help we were able to give our people!

Resignation

Settling into a coastal town instead of a remote barrio was a new experience for us. Unaccustomed as we were to city living, we had not foreseen the need for the customary bars on all windows and were consequently robbed five times before the bars were in place. This made it necessary for Bob and me to take turns house-sitting on Sunday mornings. When it was my turn at home one Sunday, I was deep into the study of Ezekiel when suddenly a verse leaped off the page. I looked up.

"Lord, are you telling us to resign from Wycliffe?" I asked. But this was too heavy for me.

"If this is really You speaking, Lord, You can tell Bob!"

With that, I firmly closed my Bible and never again looked at that passage. Nine months later Bob decided to devote a week to prayer and fasting because of a voice problem that had developed during our Manila assignment when Bob served the mission as an administrative assistant. He had lost his voice gradually over the period of that stressful year and was reduced to a whisper. This assignment in Manila had followed on the heels of the revival in OCHO and was a very difficult year indeed. During our short furlough that followed, my doctor—brother Thornton Stearns—had sent him to the finest throat specialist in New Jersey, only to learn that there was nothing physically wrong with his throat or voice.

"If you haven't recovered your voice in a year," Kway had warned him, "be sure to have it checked again in Manila," which Bob did, only to be told the same thing.

And so Bob turned to the Lord for understanding and healing. At the end of his first day of fasting, I asked, "What did the Lord say to you today, honey?"

"Well, it's strange," he answered, "but I think the Lord was saying that we should resign from Wycliffe."

"Oh, really!" I was genuinely shocked.

The next day I asked the same question and got the same reply.

"Oh, really?" I answered innocently.

At the end of Bob's third day of fasting, I repeated the same question, and when the same answer came, I said, "Are you absolutely sure?"

"Yes," he replied, and this time there was certainty in his voice.

"Well, then," I responded, "I'll show you a verse the Lord gave me back in September."

But now I couldn't find that passage of Scripture! I had never looked at it again in the nine months that had elapsed. In order to find it I had to go back to Moffatt's Translation of the Bible, which I happened to have been reading at the time. There it was. Not only was the verse underlined, but I had also written in the margin of that Bible, "June 1972." It was June 1972, nine months later! I was flabbergasted. I had no recollection of having written anything next to the verse, nor did I have a clue how I arrived at that date, and I still don't! But it was obviously the Lord's confirmation. The next morning Bob wrote his letter of resignation from Wycliffe. We had no reason to offer for resigning, except that God told us to. We were reluctant to say that, however, as God often gets blamed for things that were never His idea, so we simply resigned and left it at that.

The Lord confirmed this difficult decision over the next few years when we were pleasantly surprised to realize that Bob's translation output had doubled and his voice returned.

A Rabbit Scare

During these years in Iligan, our children were occupied with school as well as their usual pets, which always played a major role in their lives. Greig conducted a thriving and profitable poultry business and, with much self-discipline, he rose early each morning to clean the pens and feed his White Leghorns before school. I was his sole market, which meant we had freshly laid eggs for breakfast every morning and angel cakes when there was a surplus. Using much maturity and restraint, Greig banked his profits, which provided him with a handsome sum for shopping in Hong Kong on our next trip back to the States.

Keith's rabbit project was not commercial. They were his pets, although they ended up on our dining room table unexpectedly. One morning before school one of the rabbits bit him. We noticed his finger was bleeding slightly, and he explained that one of his pet rabbits was sick, so he had carried it in a cardboard box to his bedroom to better supervise its recovery. As he lifted it gently off the ground into the box, it had screeched and bitten his finger, which did not unduly concern him. Bob sensed the possible danger, however, and looked up *rabies* in Merck's medical manual. To play it safe, we went to the Seventh-Day Adventist Hospital in town and explained the situation to the missionary doctor.

"I predict the rabbit will be dead before you eat lunch this noon," Dr. Dick said gravely.

The doctor's prophecy proved accurate to the hour. When the rabbit died at noon, he immediately sent its head by plane to another island, where the lab results at a large hospital in Dumaguete later confirmed rabies. The rabbit had probably been bitten by a rat that carried the disease.

Dr. Dick started Keith that afternoon on rabies injections. The problem was, a complete series consisted of fourteen injections of imported serum, but he had only three shots on hand, and even these three had already expired. He advised us to go to a larger city, where a fresh supply might be available, and to start all over again with fourteen shots. Local serum was not only unreliable, it was downright dangerous. It was known to actually cause rabies. Several years earlier we had watched missionary parents helplessly holding their two year old child in the death throes of rabies after the child had been injected with local vaccine, while the dog in question proved to be healthy. The local vaccine had fatally induced rabies.

As soon as we got home, I began packing. Bob would stay with our other children while Keith and I would leave that evening on the overnight boat to Cebu, which was the next largest city after Manila. If we failed to find U.S. vaccine there, plan B was to fly to Manila and seek help at Clark Air Force Base. If that failed, we would have to proceed to the States. My packing was complex.

On our second day in Cebu, the supply of expired vaccine was exhausted and I was ready to book a flight to Manila that night. I had called every drug house near and far, including some in Manila, without success. No drugstore carried the imported serum. Finally, one of the Cebu missionaries suggested a certain Chinese doctor who might possibly have his own supply of rabies vaccine. I was not optimistic, but we went to his office late that afternoon out of desperation and sure enough, he had a full supply of vaccine from the States, enough for fourteen shots! He asked us not to leave Cebu for several days, however, as he had noticed a strange reaction after the first injection and wanted to observe Keith. Finally, after several days, the doctor was satisfied and sent us back to our island of Mindanao with the remaining precious vaccine. Keith was a brave camper and never once complained about the painful injections in his stomach.

In all the years we had lived in Wao and Tugaya, there had never been an emergency like that—not until we moved to a town where there was a doctor and a hospital! God is faithful!

Chapter 7

Dallas Interlude

An Idyllic Setting

Greig and Carole were now sixteen and fourteen. Having lived in the Philippines all their lives, and most of that time in the barrio with us, our children had never been part of a strong, vibrant church, and we felt they needed someone besides us to round out their spiritual development. I had also noticed a growing wistfulness in Carole. She was lonely, and Greig, too, was at an age where he needed to be with other Christian teenagers.

On the other hand, our two barefoot Tom Sawyers, Keith and Sharon, who were thirteen and nine, lived perfectly fulfilled lives in our idyllic setting. At the close of school every afternoon, they would slip into their bathing suits and grab a cookie on their way out the back door to the river, which emptied into the sea. Floating down river into the sea, they would come up on the beach and cross the road to the front of our house and plunge back into the river again, only to repeat this cycle over and over. If not swimming, Keith was tending his goats and rabbits or roaming the hills with his friends across the river. You could always see Sharon with Delilah, our spider monkey, clinging to her tummy while she played with Daisy, the other monkey, and the rest of the animals or with her neighborhood companions. We couldn't have dreamed of a more ideal setting for our younger two, but it was time to leave, and even they were soon excited by the prospect of three weeks at sea on a passenger liner.

Our neighbors asked if we would ever return. "Oh, yes, in

five years," I said flippantly, although it proved to be somewhat prophetic. We were back in four and one half years.

We told the Lord we were willing to settle anywhere He wanted us—Alaska, Hawaii, Timbuktu. For a number of reasons we had ruled out Bob's home, Seattle, which was experiencing economic depression in the early seventies with heavy layoffs at Boeing. And we weren't excited about the now-congested East Coast where I had spent my teen years. The area of Long Island where we lived during our first four years of marriage was too rich for our blood and too sophisticated for our barefoot younguns. Finally, through visiting missionary friends who hailed from Dallas, we were drawn to that city, and God sent His peace to confirm the decision.

Air travel was now competitive enough to put passenger ships out of business, and the American President Line was offering a tri-holiday discount for its final passenger voyage before converting the entire fleet to cargo carriers. Traveling by ship enabled us to take our barrels home without extra charge. After Thanksgiving in Japan, the ship docked in Manila, where we boarded for our three-week journey to the States. We celebrated a gala Christmas on board and dropped anchor in San Francisco Harbor on New Year's Day, 1973. Home of Peace outfitted us elegantly with winter clothes before we headed for Dallas.

While still on the ship, Bob and I had asked the Lord to please enable us to find "our" church right away since that was our sole reason for leaving the Philippines. Arriving in Dallas, we went directly to Christ for the Nations, where we stayed in the missionary apartment for two weeks while house hunting. It was a Saturday when we got there, and a letter was waiting for us from Margaret, a Wycliffe colleague who had just left the area. She wrote about a beautiful move of the Spirit in one of the Dallas churches, and having no better place to go the next day, we decided to check it out. What a thrill to see the enormous crowd of young people who filled the entire front half of the sanctuary.

"Look no further," the Lord spoke to both of us, and we didn't.

That January we joined Beverly Hills Baptist Church, where our teenagers fit comfortably into the landscape. These were the days of the Jesus people and the Charismatic Renewal.

Walking on Water

Bob had brought with him the entire first draft of the Maranao New Testament, which provided enough editing and refining work to keep him busy for several years to come. After eight months, however, he needed to check his work with a native speaker, which would require a trip back to the Philippines. He could make no further progress without going over every word with a Maranao.

Finding a Maranao, however, who would be willing to leave his home and travel through hostile territory to the Wycliffe base and remain there for several months of tedious work away from family and familiar surroundings would be a formidable challenge, something only God could bring about. But first Bob needed to get himself there. And so we waited expectantly for the Lord to supply the necessary funds to pay for his ticket to the Philippines. We waited all summer, in fact, but none came.

One day early in September, I asked Bob, "If money were not a problem, when would you leave?"

"The end of this month," he responded.

I phoned a travel agent and made his reservation to Seattle for the last Monday in September and an ongoing flight to Manila a few days later. The Seattle layover was to give him a few days' visit with his widowed mother on the way. Again we waited, but the mail brought no money.

The day before Bob was scheduled to leave Dallas was a Sunday, and we thought perhaps the Lord would meet the need through an offering at church. Our pastor announced in the morning service that Bob Ward was leaving the next day for the Philippines, and he led the congregation in an impassioned prayer for God's blessing and fruitfulness on that trip, but no offering was taken.

"Well, they will probably take up an offering for you tonight," I said, trying to sound reassuring. The evening service came to a close, however, with an offering taken for a couple who was being transferred by their company to a northern state, but none for Bob's trip! The service was followed by a farewell party for the same couple.

What we did not realize that day was that our pastor, along with everyone else in this Southern Baptist church, assumed that a mission board was providing our salary and taking care of all our expenses. That was their only experience with missions, but nothing could have been further from our situation.

As we filed out of the sanctuary and inched toward the fellowship hall that Sunday evening, I found myself walking next to the children's pastor, Carol Serratt, whom I knew only slightly. Striking up small talk, she asked how Bob was planning to travel to Seattle the next day. How else would anyone travel if not by plane?

"By bus," I answered, trying to sound casual. We had decided that if money did not come in for his ticket to Manila, we would gather up our pennies and buy him a Greyhound ticket as far as Seattle. God would take him the rest of the way. The truth was, however, that we didn't even have enough money for a bus ticket. We had the naïve plan of pawning our wedding silver, not realizing that cash might not be so quickly forthcoming.

As we drove home from church that evening, I was filled with an inexplicable joy, which surprised me. I began to sing lustily all the way home. The family knew that Dad was leaving the next day for the Philippines, but they had no idea he didn't have a ticket nor the means with which to buy one. Perhaps we failed in not sharing this need with them. The faith and prayers of the young can be very effective.

After our usual Sunday evening snack of cold cereal and after everyone else had gone to bed, Bob and I closed our bedroom door and dropped to our knees. Pouring out our hearts to the Lord, we began praising Him, although we weren't quite sure why. In a few minutes the phone beside our bed rang. It was Carol Serratt.

"Mel and I don't feel comfortable with Bob's traveling to Seattle by bus," she explained. "We're going to buy him a plane ticket to Seattle, and we'll bring it by in the morning."

We were speechless as we once again poured our hearts out to the Lord, this time overflowing with thanksgiving. The next morning, Carol did indeed bring us a plane ticket, but it was not one-way it was a round-trip ticket from Dallas to Seattle!

While we were recovering from shock, she asked, "How is Bob going to travel from Seattle?"

And that's when Carol Serratt learned that Bob had no ticket at all, not from Seattle, not from anywhere. She was then apologetic for not being able to do more, while we tried to express how overwhelmed we were by this incredible miracle from God.

"Don't worry about the rest of the trip," we assured her. "If the Lord has done this much already, He will certainly take care of the rest of the way."

We knew He would. He had raised our faith to an unprecedented level by this generous gift. And so Bob boarded his American Airline flight at two o'clock that afternoon without missing a beat. After he had been in Seattle a couple of days, Bob's mother realized that he didn't have a ticket to Manila. Although a widow, living on a limited income, she took him to her bank and drew out enough money for a one-way ticket to Manila. It was something she wanted to do for the Lord and for her missionary son.

Upon arriving in Manila, Bob went directly to the home of close friends of ours, the Shebleys, where he stayed for several days to take care of government red tape. The first day in town, who should he run into but a Lutheran missionary who had at one time attempted to open work among the Maranaos. He had even built a home for his family across the lake from Tugaya where we lived.

"By the way, Bob," he said, "our mission has some money set aside for Bible translation. Could you use it?"

"I believe I could!" Bob answered.

It was enough pesos to cover his travel to Mindanao, where he was able to find a language helper willing to accompany him to Nasuli and stay there for three months. Locating such a Maranao was in itself no small miracle.

Back in Dallas, Greig came to me one day and said, "I want to send Dad my tithes."

Greig had graduated from high school a year early, and was now on a valedictorian scholarship at Dallas Baptist College, earning a comfortable allowance from his large newspaper route. I mailed Greig's $200 to Bob, adding to it what I could scrape together.

It was the custom at Nasuli to provide meals for visiting missionaries, who then paid for their room and board at the office before leaving. Our friends at the base had taken good care of Bob. One family gave him their guest room and provided breakfast for three months. He ate lunch every day in another home, and the evening meal in a third. At the end of three months, when Bob went to the office to pay his bill, there was no bill to be paid! No one had turned in any charges for him. Furthermore, several of the translators gave him a gift to help him on his way. After paying his language helper's salary, he had just enough money left to buy a ticket back to Seattle. It was an excited family who met him at the Dallas airport that Christmas morning.

It was this trip that taught us to ask, when seeking God's guidance, "If money were not a problem, what would we do?" We would then make our plans accordingly, trusting our faithful God to provide, which He always has. The Lord never again, however, required us to go through such a severe test!

A Tract Distribution Trip

Three more years went by in Dallas. It was the summer of 1976, and we were spending the Fourth of July weekend in prayer and fasting. We had originally planned another camping trip with our extended family in the Ouachita Mountains of Arkansas, but our spring venture into those woods had ended in disaster, with my most severe case ever of poison ivy. The forest lost its attraction.

By holy coincidence, our house was empty of children that weekend for the first time in our family's history. Keith and Sharon were at church camp, while Greig was away on a summer job, and Carole was married and living in Oklahoma. We decided to wait on God, spending the days in His Word and prayer, listening to the Holy Spirit's voice to see if He might have something specific to speak to us about. He did.

On the last evening of our fast, we took our customary communion together. Then Bob shared what the Lord had impressed on his heart. We were to make a trip back to the Philippines, distributing a tract that he would write in Maranao. As he waited on the Lord that weekend, the details of the tract unfolded. On one side of each page would be the gospel story and on the opposite side would be pictures of our Maranao people engaged in brass making. Tugaya was the center of this cottage industry, for which Maranaos are so well known throughout the Philippines. During our early years we had taken many pictures of the entire process, so it was not hard to find ten pictures to face each of the ten pages that told the story. Bob wove the brass artisans' work into the creation narrative, followed by man's sin and God's solution to his sin—salvation through the shed blood of Jesus Christ on the cross.

We had ten thousand of these little booklets printed and carried them on the plane with us at the end of October. For three weeks we would travel around the province giving out these tracts. Larger portions of Scripture would have ended in ashes, but we felt sure Maranaos would be reluctant to burn pictures of their own people, and they were. The last picture on the back of the booklet was of the old sultan who had adopted us as his son and daughter when we first arrived in the Philippines. He was dead now, the end of a long line of powerful sultans, and his picture was valuable.

During these years in the seventies blood flowed freely between "Christians" and Muslims as the Blackshirt/Ilaga war escalated with the burning of each other's villages. Ilagas threw hand grenades into mosques on Fridays, and Muslims retaliated with wholesale slaughter and the mutilation of dead victims. This was 1976 and Westerners were no longer welcome around the Lake. We were not completely aware of the extent of the danger. The Lord hid it from us and gave us instead a host of Scriptures, assuring us that we had nothing to fear and would have His protection throughout the entire trip.

Several times we received messages from friends at Nasuli, the Wycliffe base, who were concerned for our safety and were asking us to come there first, hoping to dissuade us from going to the Lake. We did go to Nasuli, but not until after we had distributed all our tracts. We had our orders and felt a sense of urgency about this mission. When it was over and we had given away ten thousand tracts, we were then able to rejoice with our fellow missionaries at Nasuli over the Lord's direction and protection. It was obvious, moreover, that much prayer had been offered on our behalf during those three weeks. We felt it, and God did exceedingly above all that we had asked or expected.

We knew we must return to Wao as well. Although Wao is in the same province as Marawi City, to this day there is no road from the Lake directly over the mountains to Wao, which is in the very center of Mindanao. We would have to circle around the coast, traveling through three other provinces and driving back up into the mountains before re-entering the province of Lanao del Sur. Before we had always flown in and out on the mission plane, but the airstrip was gone now. After we moved out, the landing area had been plowed up for planting corn. Our only way of getting there was over nearly impassable roads with no busses or public transportation of any kind.

An SUV was what we needed, both for penetrating the Lake as well as traveling to Wao, but we knew of no one on the island of Mindanao with an SUV to spare. We did know, however, that the Lord would make a way since this project was His idea.

When we arrived in Manila to begin our trip, who should we bump into but Dick Spencer. I had written to his mother, Pearl, asking her to join us in praying about our need for a SUV. It never occurred to me that the Spencers themselves might be the answer to our prayers. As soon as Dick saw us, he informed us that we were to use the plantation SUV for the entire trip. In fact, he had it delivered to us at the Iligan airport when we landed on Mindanao!

Little did we realize at first the significance of this SUV. It not only took us to Wao and back through hostile rebel territory, but we used it all around the even more hostile Lake area. By now the "cowpath" to Tugaya had been paved, and a beautiful new hardtop road circled the Lake. This show of progress was part of President Marcos' bid for the Maranao vote. The SUV made possible much greater penetration as well as a quick getaway when the atmosphere became menacing. We parked at short intervals and hiked up and down the paths leading to the Lake, especially targeting schools, as these held the greatest numbers of literates.

In the plaza of Ramain, a barrio close to Marawi City where we least expected trouble, two young men accosted us and asked why we were distributing this literature. We explained, as we had to so many others, that it was because we loved the Maranao people that we had prepared this little book for them. The two men seemed satisfied, and as we finished handing out tracts to the people living on the plaza, we noticed that one of the young men was approaching us while the other was going toward the lake. Very cordially he invited us to leave the center of the barrio and accompany him to the lake.

"There are more Maranaos to whom you can give your little book," he said.

We smiled nervously, jumped into the SUV and took off in a cloud of dust in the opposite direction from the lake. When a Maranao encourages you to distribute Christian literature, you can be certain his intentions are evil. It was a ruse. We thanked the Lord once again for sending His angels to surround us and for providing a reliable vehicle.

We did see some of our tracts ripped up and thrown at us. In fact, one religious leader in Genasi, at the far end of the lake, angrily waved a tract in our face and said, "What are you trying to do, destroy our religion?" And then he added, "This is written very clearly. This is like bringing an atom bomb into this place!"

When we heard that, we exclaimed under our breaths, "Praise God!" The gospel is indeed God's atom bomb, the power of God for the salvation of everyone who believes. And many would believe, we were certain. In fact, we have continued to pray all these many years since then for the secret believers who we are certain are there around the Lake.

It was here in Genasi that the military commander insisted on sending an armed escort with us when we returned to Marawi that afternoon. The two soldiers assigned to us were Maranaos, and they proved very helpful. Being illiterate, they had no idea that we were distributing Christian literature. At our many stops along the way they waved their arms at people, encouraging them to take our tract. Hundreds of eager hands reached out, even tearing them from our grasp. Maranaos liked the format of the little book with pictures of their own people and the Creation story, which they recognized from the Koran.

When the religious leaders in Marawi City realized what we had done and how we had penetrated the Lake area with the Christian message, all hell broke loose. It still amazes us how the Lord blinded their eyes for over a week while we drove through densely populated areas around the Lake. After we left, reports reached us in Dallas warning us that the *imams* had promised, "If the Wards ever come back here, we will kill them."

For forty years before this, missionaries had been presenting the social gospel to the Maranaos, promising never to try and convert them, and they kept their promise. They called this pre-evangelism, but it never got beyond the "pre" stage. In contrast, Jesus said, "Go into all the world and preach the gospel."

The Marawi City *imams*, in talking about Christian missionaries, have always boasted, "They can never convert us!" Sadly, this boast has not been without grounds. On the other hand they have said, "Do *not* translate your Bible into our language!" Is this because Satan knows the power of God's Word? Indeed, it is dynamite. Because of these threats, we stayed hidden for the next three decades until the entire Bible was translated and dedicated.

When we took our little booklet to Wao, however, the reaction was entirely different. Even though our people there had rejected Jesus as Savior when He healed their sick the decade before, their attitude toward the tract was as respectful as it has always been toward us personally.

The Curtain Falls

It was on this tract distribution trip that we sensed the curtain falling on our Dallas interlude. After four years in the States, we felt our mission there had been accomplished and it was time to return to the Philippines. Each year in Dallas we had asked the Lord, "Is it time for us to return yet?" At last the answer was yes.

It was also on this trip that Open Doors invited us to join their mission in the Philippines. We were to be their "cover" for covert Bible smuggling into China. Operation Pearl was in progress that year. It was the highly successful venture of an oceangoing vessel from Manila heavily loaded with a record number of Chinese Bibles. It slipped undetected into Chinese waters and unloaded its precious cargo safely on the mainland. Open Doors wanted to be able to point to us in a remote area of the Philippines in order to divert government attention from its real purpose for being there, and so they asked us to be their representatives on the southern island of Mindanao. The timing of this invitation was perfect. We had always said we would never return without a mission board.

Once more we packed our barrels. It was a strange feeling to be leaving two of our children behind. Greig was with Uncle Sam, who would later provide an opportunity for him to finish his bachelor's degree at the college of his choice. After that the Marines would train him to fly jets, paving the way for him to become a Northwest Airlines pilot. Carole was married, and she graduated in another year with her RN before starting a family. Keith and Sharon were the only ones going back with us.

We loaded our barrels on a trailer ready to be pulled from Dallas to Houston. From there they would go by sea to the Philippines while we flew. Hours before departure, a telegram arrived: "The door to your ministry has closed," signed Open Doors!

Stunned, we asked, "Lord, are You confused?"

We had been so sure of His direction and timing, but now without a mission covering, we would not be able to get a visa to live in the Philippines. Word had just reached Open Doors of the violent Maranao reaction to our tract, and they assumed this would deter us. Furthermore, they didn't want to be responsible for our demise, and we couldn't blame them. The Lord assured us again, however, that we were right on target and that He would open the door for us.

Chapter 8

China Flashback

The Queen City of Cebu

The Lord did indeed open doors for us to return to the Philippines. When we arrived in Manila, we went directly from the airport to the pier and boarded a ship for the island of Cebu, where missionary friends, the Collinses, had graciously extended their umbrella of covering for us to get a working visa. Since they lived in Cebu City, which is more than halfway between Manila and Mindanao, it seemed best to be near them during immigration proceedings. The twenty-four hour ride on an inter-island ferry went a long way toward easing jet lag.

While sluggish government red tape lengthened into nine months, we rented a house on top of majestic Busay Mountain, overlooking the bustling port of Cebu, with its enchanting, island-dotted seascape. Cebu is queen of the islands, where Magellan first landed in 1521 and claimed the archipeligo for Spain. He was soon killed, however, on the neighboring island of Mactan, which is now Cebu's airport. Being the oldest city in the Philippines, Cebu was ruled for many years by the colorful and noble-looking descendants of Spaniards who had intermarried with the island people. Eventually, this island gave the Philippines its sublime title, Pearl of the Orient.

Bob rolled up his sleeves and went to work. He was starting to revise the entire New Testament, a project which would take three years to complete. Although Wycliffe had already cleared his New Testament for publication, he felt the translation should adhere more closely to the original Greek text, resembling more the style of the English NIV, rather than a free paraphrase.

At the end of that summer, Keith and Sharon enrolled in high school at Faith Academy, the school for MKs (missionary kids) in Manila. Meanwhile, we needed a church home. Our dialect was Maranao, but there were no churches amongst our people yet, and certainly not on the island of Cebu, which is far from Muslim territory. Not being familiar with the local Visayan dialect, we looked for an English service, which we soon found in a Chinese church.

Flashback

The moment we stepped inside Cebu Gospel Church, where the Chinese preaching was translated into English, a strange feeling of familiarity came over me. Somehow, it was like coming home. The pastor, we learned later, was a Mandarin from Taiwan. He was not preaching in Mandarin, however, but in Amoy, the dialect of Filipino Chinese. We both knew we had found our church, and although I did not understand Amoy, I was, nevertheless, carried back in time to my roots in China, where I was born and where I spoke Mandarin before English.

For twenty-seven years my parents, Thornton and Carol Stearns, had been missionaries in China. They met and married in the interior, south of Beijing, where in the city of Tsinan (Jinan today) Daddy taught orthopedics in the medical school of the large, renowned Presbyterian university, where all four of us children were born. Twice a year, Dad and Mother sponsored special evangelistic services for the students, canvassing China for the most effective speakers. One year someone suggested Watchman Nee, a name they had not heard of before. Their search ended with him, and from that time on, he was their speaker twice a year.

This was the Northern Presbyterian Mission Board. Unlike its southern counterpart, which has remained evangelical, the northern board was becoming more and more liberal in theology. Although my father had first gone to China without a personal relationship with Christ, he was challenged early on by Marie Monsen, a Norwegian missionary who lived in a houseboat on the Yellow River.

"You're lost like any sinner," she confronted him. "Just because you have been educated in the finest schools in America and came to China for philanthropic reasons, this does not save you."

Dad accepted the godly rebuke and, under deep conviction, bowed at the foot of the cross, a decision that has impacted the generations which followed. After that my parents found themselves increasingly in the evangelical camp. They rejoiced in the beautiful revival that God was sending to the students, few of whom had come to a saving faith in Christ before attending these meetings. The mission board, however, looked askance at this "emotionalism" and wished to put a stop to the meetings, which eventually led to a crisis for Dad and Mother. They could no longer remain under a board that wanted to stamp out the beautiful movement of God so dear to their hearts. As they confronted the enormity of the decision to terminate ties with their beloved mission board, there ensued for them a painful internal conflict.

Back in the 1920s, a term on the mission field was seven years. As my parents were preparing for their second furlough, the shipping company offered around-the-world passage at a rate they couldn't resist, which is how they happened to stop off in England on their way home.

In London they visited with T. Austin-Sparks, the well-known conference speaker and author who had influenced Watchman Nee's ministry. Over the years that followed, Mr. Sparks became a very close friend, making our New Jersey home his own on all his trips to the States. His daughter later married my brother, Paul. At the end of that furlough, after sixteen years under the Presbyterian board, Dad and Mother submitted their resignation and returned to China as independent missionaries.

Hardoon Road

My parents were naturally drawn to Shanghai, the home of Watchman Nee's ministry, which had so powerfully impacted their lives. Brother Nee pastored the "mother church" there and preached in Mandarin rather than the local Shanghai dialect. Mandarin was the dialect Dad and Mother were fluent in, and they took copious notes in all the services. It was a large congregation where Nee raised up countless young men, training and commissioning them to go throughout China to evangelize and plant churches. Local missionaries dubbed these churches the "Little Flock."

The Shanghai church was located on Hardoon Road, a street which took its name from a wealthy Jew who had migrated to Shanghai from the Middle East at the end of the nineteenth century. We generally referred to the church simply as "Hardoon Road." Here our family became an integral part of the Little Flock, where my father served as elder, albeit a lay leader, not clergy. He opened his own medical practice and was self-supporting during the next decade while war with Japan raged around us.

The Little Flock celebrated communion every Sunday evening in the homes of the elders throughout the city. Too young to attend these meetings at first, I have vivid memories of falling asleep Sunday nights to the melodious sounds of Chinese hymns floating up from the living room or sitting on my mother's lap during the worship.

There were summers when Watchman Nee would join us for a few days of relaxation at our seaside bungalow in Qingdao, a popular missionary resort up the coast from Shanghai. He was a tall, handsome Southerner from Fukien Province, known today as Fujian Sheng. He wore the long Chinese gown but spoke impeccable English with an Oxford accent, having been educated in England in preparation for assuming the family's chemical manufacturing business. Watchman Nee was a people person, not intense as one might imagine from his writings. He was affable and relaxed and enjoyed being with people.

Special People

We met many special people during our years in Shanghai. These were years when Jews were fleeing from Hitler's Germany. Shanghai, being an open port, was one of the few places in the world where German Jews were not turned away. They landed in large numbers, arriving with only the clothes on their backs, and were housed in refugee camps outside the city. As soon as they started coming, my parents spent every Sunday afternoon visiting in these camps, sharing Jesus with God's chosen people. Because they were special to God, they were very special to my parents as well. Our home was open, and we always had one or two of these new believers living with us while being discipled.

Michael Weiss was a young man who had embraced Yeshua as his Messiah and who lived in our home longer than any of the others. After the death of Hitler, some of these Germans remained in Shanghai to begin a new life. Michael, however, returned to his homeland, where he married a Christian girl. Years later his grown daughter made an unexpected visit to the States, surprising my parents by ringing their doorbell. What a thrill to be reconnected with Michael again!

One day in Shanghai, Dr. and Mrs. Charles Scott, dear friends of my parents from the Presbyterian compound in Tsinan, were passing through the city and had dinner with us. With them was their five year old granddaughter, Helen Scott Stam, better known as the miracle baby. Her famous parents, John and Betty Stam, had been murdered by the communists when Helen was just three months old. Miraculously, she survived after being left alone for thirty hours without food or water. Helen was only three years younger than I, and although I never saw her again, I remember her so well as she sat across the dinner table from me. Our home was a center of hospitality, and Mother was always the gracious hostess.

Japan's War with China

This was the decade before Pearl Harbor when an ambitious

Japan mercilessly pummeled a pregnable China. The Japanese vision was to incorporate all of Asia under the Greater East Asia Co-Prosperity Sphere. Out in our yard, with our Collie dog trembling beside us, we would watch the sky turn red as Japanese bombs devastated the countryside. Along with his orthopedic practice, my dad spent time in rehabilitation work among the wounded Chinese soldiers. Until we left China when I was twelve, I had never lived in a country that was not at war. A disunified China, fragmented by rivaling warlords, bled at the hands of a united and aggressive Japan, hungry for land and power.

Sensing the danger for an attractive American girl of sixteen in a city overrun with Japanese soldiers, my parents sent Anne, our eldest sibling, to the States to live with relatives for her last semester of high school before attending Wheaton College. She and Paul had attended Chefoo School, the famous British boarding school for missionaries' children, from the time they reached the age of thirteen. Kway and I, on the other hand, didn't make it before the Japanese arrived.

Homeless Chinese refugees poured into Shanghai only to have their hopes for survival snuffed out by starvation. Walking to school each morning, we would often see a baby in a garbage can or an adult corpse lying on the ledge of the water department with a rattan mat draped over the body. When we saw the mat, we knew that another desolate victim had succumbed in the cold city the night before.

More than fifty years later, when China opened its doors to tourists and Northwest Airlines inaugurated its flight into Shanghai, Bob and I made our first trip back there, compliments of Greig's passes since he was a Northwest pilot. I pointed out that same water department ledge to Bob as we tramped the city searching for my childhood home, which we found our very first day, along with my school.

Pearl Harbor

Back in 1941, at breakfast one morning, Daddy turned on

the radio as usual for the local Shanghai newscast, sponsored by Jell-O. As the radio crackled to life, a familiar voice shattered the silence with his customary, "Jell-O! Jell-O! Jell-O! This is Carol Alcott bringing you the morning news." But that was the last time we heard the heartwarming greeting of the flamboyant American broadcaster. Daddy's face turned ashen as he looked up from the radio and announced in a hoarse whisper, "The Japs have bombed Pearl Harbor." The horrified look on my father's face is indelibly etched on my memory. I had no idea what Pearl Harbor was—maybe a Chinese fishing village, or perhaps a beautiful beach resort—but I knew for sure it was a terrible thing the Japs had done. Shanghai had already fallen into their hands several years earlier, and now we were at once enemy nationals, required to wear red armbands to identify ourselves. Although the armbands were intended to humiliate the foreigners, we wore them with pride.

Chapei Civil Assembly Center

It wasn't long before Americans were rounded up and interned in a prison camp on the outskirts of Shanghai. In the meantime, my father, who never got sick and never took a vacation, was now in a hospital, very ill with pleurisy. Although he was a prisoner, he was lovingly cared for by Christian nurses from Hardoon Road. While he was in isolation at the hospital, the rest of the family was imprisoned in Chapei Civil Assembly Center, where no communication was permitted with the outside world. For the duration of our time in internment camp, Mother never knew from one day to the next whether Daddy was dead or alive.

The British, being the colonizers of Asia, were more detested by the Japanese, who imprisoned them ahead of the Americans and treated them more harshly. Because of my father's illness, we were among the very last enemy nationals to be interned.

Although there was no physical abuse at Chapei, our daily food rations left something to be desired. We ate chewy, eel-like creatures under the guise of fish. Rice was polluted by floor sweepings and creeping things, while cabbage came into camp on big truck-loads smelling like garbage. Hence, we jokingly dubbed the daily menu "fish, lice and garbage." A sense of humor was life-sustaining!

Compared to other prison camps in China, ours was cause for rejoicing. In fact, some of the guards were family men who missed their own children and enjoyed watching the boys' afternoon softball games. If a boy followed a ball over the fence, however, the guard stationed on the roof had orders to shoot.

We were uniquely blessed at Chapei to be better organized than most prison camps, with a camp president who knew how to deal with the Japanese. He started out as a prisoner at Santo Tomas in the Philippines, one of the harshest camps in Asia, but he managed to get himself sent back to Shanghai. To his surprise, our Japanese commandant turned out to be the terrible one in the Philippine Islands whom he had learned to manipulate! He maneuvered himself once again into the position of president at Chapei, which was a good thing. He could then keep the commandant under control, threatening him with losing face if he carried out the drastic measures he proposed.

In the end, my dad's illness was a blessing in disguise. Because our family was separated and Daddy seriously ill, we were placed on the priority list for repatriation. Our time in camp lasted only six months before we were included in a prisoner exchange and sent to the States on the *Gripsholm*, the Swedish ship's last wartime mission of mercy. The day we left camp was a sad one, however, for those who would languish in prison for two more years, as did a dear friend of mine, Mary Ruth, who was stricken with TB. Years later we met up again at Wheaton College, where we were classmates in the grad school. She described how the prisoners who were left behind wept bitterly as our buses pulled out of Chapei that September morning.

The *Teia Maru*

It was not the lovely *Gripsholm* which we boarded at the port of Shanghai, however. We were still prisoners of the Japanese, and the prisoner exchange had to be conducted on neutral soil. One thousand Japanese from the States would be exchanged for the same number of Americans from Asia. And so we sailed from Shanghai on a Japanese ship, the *Teia Maru*, to Marmagoa, a Portuguese port on the western coast of India. Because of the circuitous route we were on, it took a whole month for us to reach Goa, a hungry month, when food was in short ration and passengers retired at night on empty stomachs.

The *Teia Maru* was a French luxury liner that the Japanese had confiscated. It was designed for four hundred passengers. Now it bulged with a thousand souls, many of whom were crammed into the hold below. My two brothers, older than I, were assigned spaces in that hold, which had been intended for cattle, where oppressive heat made sleep impossible. The weather was accommodating, however, and along with the men, they brought their mats up on deck each night to sleep under the stars and be fanned by cool sea breezes. My father's illness was serious to the point of rating a first-class cabin, where my mother made floor space for my mat.

As we passed through the Sunda Straits, Mother called me to the bow of the ship one evening to watch the suicide boat ahead of us. The Japanese had planted so many mines in these waters that they lost track of them and had, therefore, sent the small boat ahead to be blown up instead of us in case they hit a mine. The Japanese government was not so much concerned with our wellbeing as they were in making sure that the full head count of prisoners was alive for the exchange in India. Fortunately, we sailed without incident.

The *Gripsholm*

Never in our wildest imagination could we have envisioned the welcome that awaited us in Goa by the Swedish crew of the *Gripsholm*! As we reached the top of the gangplank and stepped onto the deck that afternoon, the crew handed each person a pound-size Nestle chocolate bar. The Red Cross was on hand, also, with toys for the children and warm clothes for everyone. An hour or so later, tunes from the melodious dinner gong floated across the deck, and we were ushered into the dining saloon, where an elaborate buffet awaited us. Every eye bulged in disbelief. No smorgasbord could hold a candle to that first meal in freedom. Our parents' warning not to eat too much at first fell, of course, on deaf ears, and unfortunately, there were not a few upset tummies that night among the younger crowd, who had tried to make up in one meal for a month of hunger!

These were war years, and we sailed under the Swedish and Red Cross flags. The *Gripsholm* took six weeks to reach New York, avoiding as much of the war zone as possible and stopping at two ports along the way. At the lovely British town of Port Elizabeth, South Africa, hospitality was especially warm as the people welcomed us into their homes and took us to their white, sandy beaches for an unforgettable day of swimming, food, and fun. At Rio de Janeiro, Brazil, we roamed the city as gawking tourists and rode the famous cable car across the valley to Sugar Loaf Mountain.

Finally in December 1943, after being at sea for two and one half months, we dropped anchor in New York harbor. When my father had regained his health, our family relocated to suburban New Jersey, where once again he opened his orthopedic practice and my brother Kway and I enrolled in high school. Kway's real name is Thornton, after my father, but to the Chinese it was disrespectful to call a child by the same name as his father, and so he has always gone by his Chinese name—always, that is, with the family.

Back in the Philippines

After Bob and I spent nine months in Cebu, the government approved our immigration status and stamped the precious working visas into our passports. It was time to continue our journey farther south to Mindanao and the province of Lanao del Sur, where Maranao language assistants would be available.

Chapter 9

Return to Wao

Spiritual Warfare

Arriving on Mindanao, we made the port city of Cagayan de Oro our base. At this stage in translation, desk work could progress more rapidly in the city, with fewer interruptions than in the barrio. We worked for a month at a time in Cagayan, after which we would go to Wao for several weeks of checking, returning again to the city for another month of work. We repeated this cycle for the next five years until revisions were finished and the New Testament was ready for publication, followed by a narrative version of the Old Testament as well as a correspondence course.

The day before our first trip to Wao, Bob woke up with a stiff neck. The next morning the soreness had left his neck, but a pain had settled in his back near the left shoulder blade. Several times during each day and night that followed, the muscle went into a spasm, leaving him in excruciating pain for half an hour. The pain would then travel down his left arm, leaving a sense of numbness in his fingers and upper arm. The Holy Spirit let us know this was a demonic attack. It continued for six weeks.

The closer we got to the completion of the New Testament, the more Satan intensified his attacks, most of which focused on Bob's body. They always occurred just as we were leaving the city to go out to Wao and cleared up as suddenly as they had appeared when we returned. After that first attack, it was usually a general malaise, a feeling of great weakness all over his body, making it extremely difficult to work. The day after returning from one of these trips, Bob spent the day in prayer seeking relief from the Lord, when all at once the attack lifted and he was restored to his former good health and energy. Previous days spent in prayer, however, had not produced this same tangible result.

No one knows better than Satan the power there is in the Word of God, and he seems to have placed his top generals in Muslim areas. Christians at home held up our arms as we engaged in this spiritual warfare prior to publishing the New Testament.

A Dirge

The road to Wao was under heavy construction during those years. Engineers arrived from the farthest corners of Asia to oversee the erection of bridges that would span canyons and to repave the highway the Americans had built soon after the Spanish/American War. Today the trip from Cagayan to Wao can be covered in four hours, but in the late seventies it was an exhausting twelve-hour ordeal by bus, if we were fortunate enough to make it in one day. Heavy rains reduced the "highway" to a quagmire and washed out wooden bridges, which meant walking calf-deep through river shallows, carrying our clothes and supplies to the waiting bus on the other side.

Busses had a capacity of sixty, but with people jammed into the aisles, they usually carried more than one hundred. Flying over the deep ruts and taking mountain curves too fast, they sometimes ended up in the ravine below with only a few injured survivors left. One of these return trips from Wao prompted the following dirge:

> Jeepneys, careening down the mountain,
> Clumsy with humanity hanging outside,
> Groaning back up the far side of the ravine
> Over slippery wet rocks.
> Up and down over the lush countryside,

Through rainforests, past corn fields,
Stopping constantly to pick up another fare.
At last the highway where the busses pass,
With standing room only.
Do we let this one go by and hope for a seat on the next?
The second bus doesn't even have standing room!
Countless human cargo perched on top,
Numberless bodies hanging on to rails,
More crushed on the steps at both open doors,
Still more squeeze on!
We shrug resignedly.
Three busses later we board, standing,
Ceiling shoulder high,
An American shoulder, that is.
A mother sits on the wet, muddy floor patiently nursing her baby,
A sibling perched on her other leg.
The bus lurches. We grab our shoulder bags,
Hoisting them, struggling desperately to keep our equilibrium.
Too late—the heavy bag strikes the mother. We wince.
She cradles her head with her arm,
The nursing one hangs on by himself.
Another landslide—a baptism of mud.
The bus vomits its passengers to wade through ankle-deep slosh
While the wheels creep through, hubcaps immersed.
Another construction site. The mud is too deep.
Passengers are dumped unceremoniously,
This time to plough through the deep mire, rubber thongs in hand.
The bus does not attempt to go through.
We wait for a vehicle on the other side,

Hoping something will come before dark.
It was dawn when we left Wao.
Twelve hours later we arrive in Cagayan, bone-weary,
But the sun has not set yet!
An experience designed to produce Christian character.
The spirit rejoices and praises God,
But the flesh groans, "Lord, how long?"

Faith Academy Breaks

During these years Keith and Sharon were flying home from Manila every couple of months for their ten-day breaks from Faith Academy. We hung our calendar around these times and looked forward eagerly to their coming, with early morning snorkeling followed by breakfasts on the beach and late afternoon hikes around the crest of the nearby mountain. The problem, however, was that public transportation to the beach was nonexistent in Cagayan and taxis were few and far between back then.

While we were still living in Cebu, the Lord had promised us a car, but a whole year had elapsed without this promise being fulfilled. We reminded the Lord of this, and He assured us again that He would give us a car. Considering Keith's long legs and six-foot, four-inch frame, it would be difficult for him to fit into a two-door sedan, so we asked the Lord specifically for a car with four doors. And, because of the intense heat during the dry season, we added air conditioning to our list of specs, which meant it would have to be a fairly new car, since air conditioners didn't work in old ones. "And, Lord, would You please give it to us before the kids come home for the summer?" we added.

The only way that could happen was for a check of astronomical proportions to arrive in the mail. We waited expectantly, going daily to the post office to check our mail box. As the weeks slipped by, I finally became discouraged and my faith shrank to a new low. There was only one week left before Keith and Sharon would be home again, and it would take longer than that to change a dollar check into pesos at the bank.

"Oh, don't give up now!" Bob exhorted.

The next morning, with his Bible tucked under his arm and a bottle of water in the other hand, Bob left home to spend the day in prayer by the creek. As evening shadows crept across the sky, he returned and announced with absolute certainty, "The Lord is going to give us a car."

"But it can't be before the kids come home," I thought. The day arrived, and I mounted the motorcycle behind Bob for the ride to the airport. We were happy to see our children again and exuberantly masked our disappointment over not having a car. Keith rode home with Bob on the motorcycle while Sharon and I thumbed a ride back to town with friends.

That afternoon I made the usual welcome home pizza, which was still in the oven when Gubby, our vigilant German Shepherd, started barking. Who was at the gate but Benny and Jenny, our dear Chinese friends! Benny's older brother, George, was a good friend from the Chinese church in Cebu.

"You must stay and eat pizza with us!" I urged.

As we visited in the *sala* after supper, Benny pulled something out of his pocket.

"George said to give you this," he said, dangling a pair of car keys.

George was the owner of a prosperous Mitsubishi sales company on the island of Cebu, and Benny managed the Cagayan branch. The keys were to a Lancer that had been used as a demo for only a few months. It was a practically brand new 4-door sedan, with a powerful AC!

"It's yours for as long as you need it," Benny was saying. Bob and I were so stunned we were having trouble putting words together. This was still the very day the kids had arrived home! God was not one day late! What an object lesson in faith for all of us, including Benny and Jenny.

As we climbed into bed that night, the thought crossed my mind, "That's the best pizza I ever made."

The Ganaban House

Our first house in Wao, the bamboo one near the airstrip, was long gone. It had collapsed with age and, of course, there are no rental houses to be had in the barrio. It was time to build again, and our headman, Datu Tao, assigned us land on the other side of the village, high up on the mountaintop.

While building was in progress, we rented the only unoccupied structure in town, totally ignorant of its history. We knew it had been built as a clinic by a doctor who had moved away, but we didn't know that he had been run out of town because of the high death rate on his operating table. With more courage than prudence, he had ventured into surgery, lacking both training and a license. There was no electricity in Wao, and the good doctor owned no generator or lab, nor did he have an anesthetist. His only assistant was his untrained sister. As his record of failure soared, so did the ghost stories.

The building was definitely haunted. There was a comfortable apartment above the clinic, which is why we rented the vacant building. One of the first things we noticed were the bamboo crosses over each doorway, where the blood of a chicken or pig had been smeared on top of the cross. This was a common symbol of the syncretism of animism and the local version of Christianity. Seeing the bloodstained crosses, we knew our job of exorcism was cut out for us. Following the words in Revelation that they overcame Satan by the blood of the Lamb and the word of their testimony, (Revelation 12:11) we exorcised each room, appealing to the sacrifice of Jesus when His blood was shed on the cross, providing victory over death and Satan. As we asked God to replace the evil spirits with His presence, He did just that.

A few days after we moved into the Ganaban house, which borrowed its name from the doctor, Datu Tao visited us, accompanied by his three wives. He had acquired a new young wife to replace my dear friend, Taraga, who had been killed by an Ilaga bomb thrown into the mosque. Tangki, the new one, was not more than a teenager, younger than some of his granddaughters. I had invited them for the noon meal and had cooked up my best Wao menu, which included the rare treat of ground beef. Not realizing that we spoke Maranao, Tangki muttered to the others that it all looked like vomit. I couldn't help smiling, as I recalled earlier similar reactions of my own to the strange-looking native food. A few years after this, Tangki ran away with a young husband who had recently married a much older woman. When I asked the young man why he had married someone old enough to be his mother, he replied, "It is my fate!" although the real reason was probably that she commanded very little dowry. Although Datu Tao knew which city the young couple had fled to, he chose to overlook the crime, probably because he realized the futility of retaliation in the light of his advancing age.

"Do you not hear noises in this house at night?" Datu Tao asked with genuine concern for our well-being.

We explained, as we had to so many others, that there is power in Jesus' name. Even Satan trembles when he hears it, we told him, and when we receive Christ as our Savior, the Holy Spirit comes to live inside of us, and He is more powerful than all the demons in hell. So why should we be afraid?

"In fact," I added, "because Jesus is inside us, Satan is afraid of us." That brought the house down, although no humor was intended.

"The ghosts are afraid of the Americans!" they roared as the Datu slapped his knee.

Our Second Wao House

Soon Ramadan would be upon us, the annual month of "fasting," when all true followers of Muhammad feast on two sumptuous meals during the night, but fast during the day, abstaining not only from food, but also from drinking water or even swallowing their own saliva. Work is at a lower ebb during this time, and we were racing with the calendar, hoping to have our house finished so we could move in before the long fast began, which we did.

The idyllic panorama at our new site was breathtaking. We were high up, overlooking a lush valley with the almost tangible beauty of deep cyanic mountains rising majestically on the other side, framing the elegant masterpiece of an artist's dream. Built high off the ground again, with most of the wall space taken up by wooden-louvered windows, our little cabin resembled a tree house—and wasn't much bigger. Sitting on the upstairs porch, one felt like a bird perched on the highest branch of a giant tree nestled in a mango grove.

Storytelling Under the Mango Tree

Our house was made from hand-sawn lumber cut fresh from the forest near the valley where we drew water when the dry season emptied our rain tank. There was a visiting area below, and each of us had a study on either side of it. Most of our time with the people, however, was spent out under the trees, wherever a cluster of Maranaos had gathered to discuss the harvest, lack of rain, the latest killing, the movement of Muslim rebels in the nearby forests, or the continuing health of someone who had been healed ten years earlier.

One day, while Bob was at the translation desk, I was sitting under a neighbor's tree visiting with the wife of a TB patient when Datu Tao came along and joined us for a chew—betelnut, that is. I abstained. Soon a group had gathered, all talking earnestly about the hunger season, which was the result of the drought. I prayed silently. Jesus always met people at the point of their need, and the immediate need was for food, specifically rice.

I asked them if they would like to hear a story. Barrio people love a good story, and my audience hung on every word as I told how Jesus took five loaves of bread and two fish and fed five thousand people, who ate until they were full. This was indeed a good story. Datu Tao punctuated it with expertly aimed spittle and frequent exclamations, which the others echoed. Then I related a recent incident of answered prayer from our own lives.

"Now," I said, "why don't you pray to Jesus about your need for rice?"

Although that was a novel idea, it seemed like a good one to the hungry group. I promised that Bob would lead them in a prayer to Jesus on the condition that they were all in agreement. Datu Tao promptly suggested Friday noon in the mosque, since that was the following day and everyone in the barrio would be together. The implications were mind-boggling. The headman had decreed that everyone in the all-Muslim village was to pray to Jesus in the mosque on Friday and be led in that prayer by the Christian missionary!

Bob and I had been praying a lot during that time about Jesus' instructions to feed the poor. The previous month we had bought a sack of rice for the barrio. After counting our pesos this time, we found we had enough for four sacks. That would feed the village for two days.

Friday arrived. I wore the head covering, and we removed our shoes along with everyone else before entering the mosque. After the opening rituals concluded, the men motioned to Bob who got up and spoke to a captive audience. He read the entire story of Jesus feeding the five thousand from his translated Scriptures, after which he offered an impassioned prayer to God in the name of Jesus.

Before sitting down, Bob told the spellbound congregation that he and his wife represented the disciples of Jesus in the story and that we were going to buy four sacks of rice for them, which would symbolize the bread and the fish. He announced that he was going to pray again, asking Jesus to bless those four sacks of rice and multiply them so that no one would be hungry again throughout the rest of the drought until the next harvest. Muslim ritual has everyone raising his arms during prayers. As Bob led in this second prayer, every arm was lifted and the atmosphere, electric. Bob sat down and the Datu jumped to his feet talking excitedly, ignoring the *imam* behind him who was chanting the Arabic prayers.

After that, events took place in staccato-like succession, events that could not possibly be labeled "chance."

That same week one of the men collected the government insurance on his soldier son who had been killed in a skirmish a few months earlier. It was an enormous sum of cash by barrio standards, and he quickly became the Wao Loan Association, providing ready cash to be repaid at harvest time with the usual 100 percent interest, of course. From the moment our four sacks of rice were consumed, the people were able to borrow this money for food and were never hungry again during the entire drought. We lost no opportunity in reminding them that this was God's answer to prayer offered in the name of Jesus.

The Favor of God

Although there were no mass conversions, the Lord was giving us favor in Wao, which was vital to our continuing presence in that turbulent region.

A few weeks later, just hours before we returned to Wao again, Datu Tao had announced that their corn and rice crops would all be lost if rain didn't fall by the next day. Hydroelectric plants, which supplied most of the nation's power, had either been shut down or cut back to 50 percent output throughout the islands as water levels in rivers and lakes dropped to an all-time low. That evening when we arrived back in Wao, it poured. This was only a few hours after Datu Tao's doom-filled pronouncement!

"It is because you are back that Allah sent us rain," was the consensus amongst the village elders the following day.

Securing our shoulder bags as we stepped off the bus in Wao the day before, we had stopped to chat with the town mayor's daughter.

"My mama has just delivered seventy two sacks of rice to your barrio," she said, informing us of the government aid to the drought-stricken rural areas.

Seventy-two sacks! That was enough to feed the whole barrio for more than a month! And this was to be repeated on a monthly basis until the next harvest. With full stomachs, the people greeted us joyfully. Once again we had arrived in the wake of good news. It had happened too many times for even a skeptic to miss the divine connection. Favor! God had granted us favor with our Maranao people, as only He could do. No missionary with a bold evangelical witness can remain in a pure Maranao community without His favor.

"When you are here, it is peaceful," Mayimuna observed wistfully, making reference to the numerous killings that had taken place in our absence.

"If you had been here, my husband would not have died," declared old Odao.

"Your prayers are very effective," Rambanayan, the barrio midwife, remarked as she came asking us to pray for her sick neighbor.

"Your medicine is very powerful," Abdullah observed thoughtfully as we gave him two ordinary aspirin.

The climax to all of this came when the Datu invited Bob to preach the Friday sermon in the mosque!

It is customary for Muslims to invite a visitor to deliver the sermon, and Datu Tao was singularly broad-minded. What a golden opportunity! Sensing that such an occasion might never again present itself, Bob prepared night and day for this incredible event. His sermon was his testimony of what God had done for him through His Son, Jesus Christ, who died on the cross to pay for his sins and rose again to live forever. He told of his assurance of eternal life in heaven with God, something no Muslim can ever be sure of. As much as Maranaos love to argue, no arguments followed. It's hard to dispute someone's personal experience. I would dearly love to conclude this episode by saying the entire community turned to Christ en masse, but that did not happen.

The New Testament Is Published

After three years of revising the New Testament, Bob was finally satisfied.

With less paraphrasing, his updated translation conformed more to the original Greek texts. And so, with his precious manuscript tucked securely under his arm, we boarded a ship in Cagayan for the overnight trip back to the island of Cebu, where three thousand copies were printed. When it came off the press a year later, Fred, one of the missionaries who had arrived the previous decade, showed it to his Maranao friends.

"Who wrote this book?" they would ask him.

"An American," was Fred's answer, careful not to divulge Bob's name.

"No, this could only have been done by a native Maranao," they insisted, and the religious leaders made it a high priority to locate the Muslim who had committed the crime against Allah of translating the Christian holy book. The people from the Lake refused to believe that an American had been responsible, and the political and religious leaders became increasingly determined to find the guilty Muslim. To kill him would be doing Allah a favor. To this day we have guarded the identity of every Maranao who has ever helped check the translated Scriptures.

Bob's next project was to translate the widely used correspondence course, *One God, One Way*, followed by a complete narrative version of the Old Testament from Hurlbut's Bible stories. That was his last project before acquiring his first computer in 1983.

The Rebels

By this time Muslim rebels had swarmed into the hills surrounding Wao, making forays into our barrio. Officially, the rebels were fighting to gain control of the entire island of Mindanao as part of their goal to secede from the Philippines. Most of them, however, were nothing more than hoodlums-turned-bandits, with no lofty aspirations. They were making a living in whatever way they could, and kidnapping was especially lucrative. From our Wao porch, nestled high up among the branches of a mango grove, we could see them coming down the trail into the barrio, eyeing us all the while. Although we were still under Datu Tao's protection, he came to us one day with an ominous warning.

"Never open your door at night, even if the voice is mine!"

We did not take lightly our angelic protection in this troubled area, where rebel cooking fires lit up the forest at night, and while the threat of the *imams* on the Lake to kill us if we ever returned continued to ring in our ears. We lived on the promises of God, and with those we felt as secure as we would have anywhere else in the world. Nevertheless, we knew our time in Wao was drawing to a close.

Chapter 10

Maguindanao, a Second Translation

Ambushed

"Come over here," Bob's low, muffled voice kept calling from the shallow ditch beside the coastal road we'd been traveling on a few minutes before.

I was sprawled on the ground half under our SUV, eyeing the high barbed-wire fence that separated us. Afraid to go over the top because of the heavy gunfire and loud explosions all around, and not sure I could get under it, I kept crawling farther away under the SUV.

We were living in Cotabato, translating for the Maguindanao, and had driven four hours to the coast to have a weekend of much-needed rest by the sea before the final push of preparing the four Gospels for distribution. We were trying to get home in time for my Sunday afternoon Bible class with college students in Cotabato.

The coastal city of Davao, where we had gone for our break, was an hour behind us when we heard shooting up ahead. We were following a truck carrying large tanks of bottled gas. The passenger jeepney ahead of the truck made a fast U-turn and we followed suit, wanting to get away as quickly as possible from the explosive cargo in front of us.

At a safe distance back, we stopped to wait out the shooting. Suddenly it was coming closer. We dove back into the SUV, and Bob drove with his foot hard against the floorboard, praying that we would make it back to Davao ahead of the violence. It wasn't long, however, before we came to a roadblock. Several vehicles that had been going in the direction of Davao had tried to turn around, just as we had done, when they heard the volley of bullets in the opposite direction. They were parked across the road completely blocking all traffic. The firing was now coming from both directions. In fact, it was all around us.

"Duck!" I yelled. But Bob didn't think the SUV was much protection.

"We've got to get out of here," he said rushing out his side, around to my side, and through the barbed wire into the ditch, while I slid out my door onto the ground and inched away from the ditch and further under the SUV. As Bob kept calling from his foxhole, however, I knew I *had* to get through that barbed wire. Any minute we might need to make a dash for it into the jungle toward the sea. Plunging beneath the lowest rung of wire, half expecting to leave my dress behind on the barb, I landed in the ditch beside Bob and another "refugee," who turned out to be a believer. The three of us prayed. We learned later that just a month before this, the communist NPA (New People's Army) had held up this woman's rubber plantation and butchered her husband before her eyes!

Although we were completely outside of Muslim reach, we were in the area where communist activity was at its height. During the short lull that followed, the young NPA soldiers, one of them a girl, began searching the cars for weapons and anything else of value. We were watching from the ditch a few feet away as they opened our SUV. Not wanting our presence to startle the heavily armed rebels, Bob decided it was better to face his murderers than to take a shot in the back.

"Sir, what are you looking for?" Bob said gently.

Terrified lest they shoot him, I jumped up and, pointing frantically at Bob, screamed, "*Padre*!" meaning "Reverend father."

This was the closest term to *missionary* that I could think of in their Visayan dialect, which was not familiar to us. I was simply trying to distract them.

The young revolutionary swung around, "*Padre*?"

"Yes," answered Bob.

Turning to me with wide eyes, he asked, "*Madre*?" or "Reverend Mother."

"Yes," I responded. These were the terms the barrio people used in greeting us back in the good old days when it was safe to hike in the mountains.

Quickly he shouted to his companion, who was rummaging through our SUV, "*Padre*! *Madre*!"

The second soldier stared at us incredulously, "*Padre*? *Madre*?"

"Yes."

He slammed the door shut, leaving everything intact.

They ordered us to cross the road to a safer place, and as we scrambled out of the ditch, the first boy said to me in broken English, "I rebel."

Eyeing his loaded armalite, I smiled feebly while Bob took advantage of the moment to lock our SUV.

As Bob joined us, the boy added, "You no angry I rebel?"

"Oh, *no*!" we chorused, shaking our heads vigorously and smiling nervously again at the enormous guns. Actually, we were terrified!

The VIP treatment we were getting was due to the Catholic Church's participation in the communist revolution in the Philippines. Although not intentional on our part, the terms *Padre* and *Madre* had aligned us with their cause!

The little farmhouse on the far side of the road was made of solid concrete, which is unusual for farmhouses on Mindanao, shielded as the island is by a myriad of smaller ones, which protect it from the devastating typhoons that ravage the exposed northern island of Luzon. We huddled on the floor along with the passengers from the jeepney that had been ahead of us and waited tensely for an hour while bullets whizzed all around us. The incessant firing was interspersed by deafening explosions, which we later learned were a total of five vehicles being blown up by land mines, two of them busses that had, fortunately, been emptied of passengers. The rebels were not just slaughtering innocent civilians this time, as they sometimes do in ambushes like this when they fire indiscriminately into a busload of people.

It was from the jeepney passengers that we learned the provocation for the ambush. Traveling in their party just ahead of them was the mayor of one of the neighboring towns who had been a communist rebel. No one leaves the NPA without paying a high price for betrayal, and the angry communists were now attempting to exact that price and, while they were at it, to confiscate as many guns as possible from his armed escorts.

From news reports we learned later that the mayor and three of his policemen had been badly wounded but did manage to make it to a hospital in time, while a six year old boy and his mother were caught in the crossfire and had not been as fortunate. Foiled in their attempted revenge, the enraged NPA vented their fury by terrorizing the countryside in a display of strength.

Suddenly the shooting stopped. We waited another hour, this time in oppressive silence, while no one dared venture out for fear that the NPA might still be around. At last, when all was safe, the army arrived. It had taken them nearly three hours to respond! It was all right to go back to Davao now, they told us, but not to Cotabato, where we were originally headed. The battalion was moving toward Cotabato, however. Suddenly the lieutenant had an afterthought.

"You follow us," he offered magnanimously.

"Oh, *no!*" Bob and I shook our heads vehemently.

We were not about to plunge headlong into an all-out battle. As it turned out, traffic was completely blocked on the Cotabato side for the rest of that day and night. We returned instead for another night of peaceful sleep by the sea, grateful to the Lord who had kept us safe in the midst of the storm. Once again He had been our refuge, and we were reminded of the comforting promises of protection He had given us before our trip. This was the first time in all those years, however, that we were aware of divine protection from a danger other than Muslims!

Eventually the exasperated citizens of Davao City rose up to defend themselves against the communists, forming a citizens' watch, which proved more effective than the military.

A Second Language

Our Maranao New Testament was published by this time, and Wao was a closed chapter. We were now living in the neighboring province of Cotabato, home to another large Muslim group, the Maguindanao. The two dialects are very closely related, with more than fifty percent overlap in vocabulary, yet they were not close enough to share the same translation of the Bible.

"When I finish translating Maranao, I'm going to do the Maguindanao," Bob had said when we first settled on the Lake and learned how similar the two dialects were. Twenty years later we were ready to do just that.

Cotabato, home of the Maguindanao, was the birthplace of Islam in the Philippines, where the first two Arabs pulled their dinghy onto the sandy shores of Mindanao in the fourteenth century. They were seafaring traders who convinced a group of pagans that they could have numerous wives and look forward to an eternal paradise of sensual pleasures if they would observe a few simple tenets. The new religion took off like wildfire.

Cotabato was also the birthplace of the Blackshirt/Ilaga conflict, and it was still reeling from the effects of war. There was only one other missionary couple there at this time, Jay and Betty Abrams, but they were living within the city and working amongst the non-Muslim population. Wycliffe had tried four times since the fifties to place translators in Cotabato, but for good reasons, each one had left.

We found a house for rent in a Muslim barrio outside the city, which meant it did not enjoy military protection, but we were used to that. Before we were settled into our new home, we wandered outside to get acquainted with our neighbors and to start learning the dialect. The very first person we came across was a friendly, educated Muslim.

"Don't go beyond the coconut tree," he warned.

When a non-Muslim warns about danger, you shrug and keep going. But when a Muslim warns you not to penetrate his territory, intruder beware! The jungles were crawling with "rebels" who, for the most part, were nothing more than bandits who had discovered the lucrative potential in kidnapping. This warning put us under virtual house arrest for the entire four years we lived in Cotabato.

Our Visayan landlady had assigned an enormous brute of a man to guard our house at night, although we did not realize until much later that we were under his watchful eye. Shots ringing out at night from the surrounding forest punctuated the peaceful concert of cicadas, producing a disturbing cacophony. We were prime targets for kidnapping, making periodic R & Rs necessary to maintain a modicum of sanity.

A few weeks after arriving in Cotabato, typhoid struck. Fortunately, only one of us succumbed, and Bob was a patient nurse. According to our medical manual, it was paratyphoid, which is more sudden and intense. Not knowing where to look for competent medical help, I had no relief from the high fever which raged unbroken for two weeks, leaving my legs weak as wet noodles.

Once again we found ourselves living in a haunted house. For many years it had been used as a gambling den as well as a place for storing illegal guns and ammunition. The Philippines was under martial law, and President Marcos had outlawed privately owned weapons. Our "Christian" landlady, however, in a complete lack of loyalty, had sold arms to the Muslims during the Blackshirt/Ilaga war the decade before. It was a lucrative enterprise, which gave her a safe sanctuary in an otherwise hostile environment.

In the middle of the second week of typhoid, we remembered we had neglected to cleanse our house when we moved in. Once again, we went through each room driving out the evil forces and filling each one with the Holy Spirit's presence. That very day the relentless pounding of my typhoid headache lifted, never to return!

A Maguindanao Wedding

I was still convalescing and weak when a familiar sound from the barrio penetrated the air. It was a kolintong, the percussion instrument consisting of seven brass gongs of graded size, signaling either a Muslim wedding or a funeral. Both of these occasions offered unparalleled opportunities for practicing the language as well as making friends and gaining deeper insights into the culture. Best of all, they provided openings for a Christian witness. We lost no time in joining the festivities, which turned out to be a wedding.

We arrived just in time for the dancing camels, a man pulling wires inside each make-believe animal. We had never seen this done in Wao, but it proved to be a standard opener for a Maguindanao wedding and was always followed by boy dancers. Next came the food trays, their bearers balancing the precious delicacies high in the air. This was part of the dowry that the groom must pay for his bride, in addition to a carabao or two, while the remainder is paid in cash.

Where was the groom? We wondered. The bride's father informed us that the couple would await the arrival of the barrio captain before the actual ceremony took place. An hour later we learned that the groom would fetch the bride from her parents' home sometime after high noon. Wearily we trudged home for a brief respite from the scorching sun and to snatch a quick bite of lunch before starting out again. We were thankful for all the new friends the Lord was giving us and the doors that were swinging open for the Gospel.

Back at the scene, the dancing camels were coming down the trail again, and this time the bride and groom followed close behind the boy dancers. The girl was only fifteen and the boy, not much older. Dressed in her colorful finery, the bride hung her head shyly, trying to conceal her blushing face behind her veil. Ascending the gaily-decorated bamboo platform, the pair sat on a bamboo sofa where bridal attendants hovered over them with fans waving incessantly and umbrellas shielding them from the tropical sun.

The *imam* and elders were already on the platform to offer prayers to Allah in Arabic and to deliver interminably long speeches laced with wise counsel. In a Maguindanao wedding the groom stands, extending his right hand, and clasps the right hand of the specified elder. There they stand facing each other for more than an hour throughout the orations. When the speeches end, the unclasping of the hands signifies that the couple is now man and wife. No kissing in a Muslim wedding! Instead, they looked to Bob to take their picture, a copy of which would be our wedding gift.

Solemnly the couple leaves the platform and proceeds to the bridal chamber, the room they will occupy for the next few months. The crowd turns its attention once again to the dancing camels, and the ritual is repeated. This is a double wedding!

The Fast of Ramadan

The festivities were over just in time for Ramadan, the month of obligatory abstinence from food and drink, perfume and sex, tobacco and betelnut chewing, and alcohol, this last one forbidden at all times for Muslims. Ramadan is definitely not the time for a wedding, even though nights are filled with feasting.

Throughout the month of Ramadan, as soon as the sun has set each evening, Muslims eat a light meal, which is followed by prayers. About an hour later, they eat again, a large meal this time, with more prayers. At two o' clock in the morning the call from the mosque awakens the barrio. It's time to rise and cook the last meal which must be finished before dawn. After that, neither water nor even one's own saliva may pass down the throat until sunset. Hence Ramadan is a month of weakness and exhaustion with very little work accomplished.

By observing the fast of Ramadan, the Muslim is seeking absolution from sins, past and future. The more suffering and privation endured during this month, the more disposed Allah will be to overlook offenses and permit entrance into eternal paradise. Although the Muslim is working hard during this time to compensate for his sins and obtain inner cleansing, he can never be sure that he will actually gain entrance into heaven. Keeping this fast, therefore, becomes a key to earning one's salvation, which explains the great emphasis placed upon Ramadan throughout the world of Islam.

It was during the month of Ramadan that the Koran began to be "revealed" to Muhammad. Prior to this revelation, it was a holy month for pagan Arabia. When Muhammad designated it as a month of fasting, he was influenced by the example of ascetic discipline among the early Christians as well as by the Jewish fast of the Day of Atonement. As time passed, however, Muhammad grew at odds with the Jews, and he studiously rejected their traditions. The Day of Atonement fast was abandoned for one of a month's duration. Thus the fast of Ramadan is at once a product of and reaction against Jewish practice.

The Kandoli

The middle of Ramadan is marked by a special night of celebration. Any Filipino Muslim who can afford it holds a *kandoli,* a feast of thanksgiving to Allah for having helped him through the first half of the fast and a prayer for grace to complete the second half. The feast is followed by the giving of alms, even if only a token amount.

We were privileged in Cotabato to be invited to the home of a wealthy Muslim for his mid-Ramadan *kandoli*, a rare invitation for an outsider. Because his home was deep in the jungle, which was now in the very heart of rebel territory, we were assigned a family member as an escort and bodyguard throughout the evening.

Arriving at seven o'clock that night, the car we rode in burst abruptly into a huge clearing and parked in front of a well-varnished, prestigious-looking house. We were ushered into an expansive room where the first light meal and prayers were already over. Seated on the sofa along with a few important relatives, we were served coffee and Maguindanao delicacies—crepes wrapped around sweet coconut paste. Household servants were placing low tray tables laden with food all around the enormous room, which soon filled up with men. The women ate later, outside. Crowding in, the men positioned themselves densely on the floor around the trays of food, leaving precious little breathing space. Using much restraint, they offered lengthy Arabic prayers from the Koran in unison before devouring the meal.

The food was highly spiced and flecked with tiny pieces of goat, chicken, and shrimp to flavor the rice. No one minded the fact that it was stone cold by this time, since little priority is placed on the temperature of food anywhere in the Philippines. It took only a few minutes to empty the trays, and soon the room was thick with cigarette smoke, which stung our eyes and choked our lungs.

It was close to midnight by the time we said farewell. Many of the guests remained for the night to sleep briefly on the floor before it was time for the last meal before dawn. It had been an evening rich in culture, and we felt honored to have been allowed to observe it. For a few hours the curtains had parted, and we were permitted a glimpse into the inner circle of Islam.

Informants

During our Cotabato sojourn, Bob had a string of language helpers, known in translation circles as "informants" before that term became politically incorrect. The first was Gandawali, a leading Maguindanao elder, who enjoyed respect from "Christians" as well as Muslims. He was well educated and taught introductory courses in Islamics at the local Notre Dame High School. This was election season, however, and Gandawali played an active role in politics, a dangerous game that resulted in serious threats to his life. Since we lived some distance from the city where foul play could easily be executed, his wife accompanied him to our house each week so as to be on hand in case he was shot. At the same time, he was under pressure from Muslim leaders because of his involvement with us. Finally, when two of his grandchildren died of measles, he interpreted it as an ill omen and quit. Who could blame him?

Bob's next language assistant was Ngoah, pronounced like Noah of the Bible. He had the rare distinction of being a believer, albeit a secret one. He had been a longtime friend of Jay, the missionary in town who had paid for his eye operation. Gratitude and indebtedness, along with pressure from Jay, motivated Ngoah to work with Bob, although fear, understandably, stalked his footsteps. He faced an incredible journey to reach our house each week, coming down river by boat. He would rise soon after midnight to ride the only launch that arrived in Cotabato by dawn. Finally, one day Ngoah failed to show up for his weekly day with Bob, and we never saw him again.

Once more the search was on for a language assistant. We made forays into surrounding areas in search of a man willing to risk his soul working on the Christian holy book. One day the Lord led us to a fishing village, and there on the beach we came across Naguib, who turned out to be God's man for the job. He had to travel nearly two hours to reach us each week, but that proved to be his protection. No one from his barrio knew where he was going when he left home every Monday morning. They assumed he was headed for the market in town to simply idle away the hours as so many men did.

According to our arrangement with Naguib, he was to eat breakfast before leaving home, but since it was not in his culture to eat at 4 a.m., I would serve him my special breakfast of Spanish egg-bread with strong, syrupy coffee. Although he lived by the sea, Naguib was a farmer, not a fisherman. He wasn't used to long, sedentary hours, and without the stimulation of physical exercise to keep him awake, his head would soon begin to nod. I stayed close by throughout the day with more strong coffee, which was only effective for a short time. Knowing the difficult trip he had to endure and the risk he was taking in coming, I would produce my most enticing menus, for which Naguib was always appreciative.

Naguib was probably the most faithful helper who ever worked for Bob. Born with a deformity, he walked with a limp. His left hand and arm were shriveled and his left leg lame, but what he lacked physically was compensated for by a keen mind and an astute grasp of concepts. Although he came from a remote place, often sloshing through seven kilometers of mud to meet his jeepney ride, he never once missed a Monday with Bob. Even during Ramadan he came, without cigarettes, refusing lunch, coffee, snacks, and water. His discomfort was probably what kept him awake.

I, too, had a language helper in Cotabato. Her name was Ding Kong, or Dings for short. She was a schoolteacher who came on Saturdays from the nearby barrio to help me with language learning and to give feedback on Bob's latest translated Scriptures. Her husband kept a watchful eye on her, however, and finally forbade her to come because of the dangerous nature of the work, which was threatening her eternal soul. After an absence of several months, however, Dings surprised us by appearing in our doorway one Saturday.

I had asked Dings the very first day she came to work with me, "What would you do if your husband decided to take another wife?"

"Oh, that could never happen," she shot back, knowing how the rest of the world views polygamy. "We are both educated, and we have an agreement that we would never do that!"

Dings and her husband did appear to have an unusually successful marriage. Their relationship seemed to be set apart from other Muslim marriages, in most of which the wife is little more than valuable property, and sometimes not so valuable. In contrast to most Muslim marriages, this one had not been arranged for them. Instead Goms, Dings' husband, had been her secret childhood admirer, who determined in his heart to marry his fair lady when he grew up. When I heard Ding's story, I wondered if perhaps this once a Muslim man had made a lifelong commitment to one woman.

Ours was a typical barrio, where the "bamboo telegraph" disseminated news rapidly. A few days before Dings returned to work, our Visayan landlady told me that Goms, in good Islamic tradition, had recently taken a second wife. When he returned home with his bride, Dings greeted him in not so good Islamic tradition—with a loaded gun! She had been betrayed, and the experience was both humiliating as well as painful. As soon as she came back, I raised her salary and we went to work in earnest.

Those Maguindanao Scriptures were Bob's first translation done with the help of a computer, which saved many hours of typing and retyping.

Trips to Wao

Wao was never far from our hearts, which is why we made several trips back there from Cotabato, although the journey was more difficult since we were on the other side of the island. By this time we had our own SUV, which meant we did not have to endure public transportation, but the drive was longer and there was a river to cross halfway there, with no bridge spanning it. We depended on a government-run ferry, which frequently shut down for repairs for several days at a time without warning. With only a four-vehicle capacity, the ferry plied the river while vehicles waited in line for an hour. Then it was catch-as-catch-can while we took a flying leap in four-wheel drive with the prayer that our wheels would catch the ferry planks at the right angle. Disembarking on the other side after a five-minute ride, Bob would gun the motor as the SUV took a flying leap before crashing down on the river bank, leaving us to wonder how long the SUV's shocks could hold up, not to mention our shattered nerves!

Three more hours through no-man's land with numerous detours brought us to the Wao turn-off, followed by another three hours over bumps and ruts and one-lane bridges about to collapse. Sometimes the only way across was through the raging river when a bridge had already caved in. Saving the best for last, we would creep up the rocky mountain road for an hour, with the fervent prayer on our lips that the Lord would hold back the rain until we reached the top, which He always did. Once the stones were wet, it would be impossible for even a four-wheel-drive SUV like ours to grip those slippery rocks, and if we didn't reach Wao before dark, it would mean overnighting somewhere in a barren wayside inn while our aching bodies longed for our own bed in Wao.

We did, indeed, have a crude refuge in the town of Maramag, which our grown son, Greig, on one of his trips back, dubbed "The Maramag Hilton." Although rat-infested, it boasted wooden beds of sorts. It was conveniently located in the very heart of Mindanao, and more than once we found sanctuary there.

Finally, just before dark, we would creep into Wao with the whole barrio turning out to welcome us home. A week with our people was well worth the trip. Friends with hacking coughs and spitting blood came for more TB medication. Aches and pains ranged from rheumatism to malaria, from ulcers to measles, as well as the ever-present dysentery. Most of them we could help at least a little, but no one was turned away empty-handed, even if we only had aspirin or sulfa-guanidine to offer.

Wherever we went on those roads, we always carried a two-day supply of food and water since we never knew when we might encounter a collapsed bridge or engine trouble, which might hold us back for a night or two. Refreshing meal-stops buoyed our flagging spirits as we sat on a log enjoying lunch in a secluded forest glen, relaxed in a cool breeze beside a river, or munched sandwiches on the crest of a knap overlooking a lush valley. Sometimes we cooled off with an after-lunch swim under tumbling waterfalls in the forest.

New Missionaries Pour In

Shortly after we settled in Cotabato, new missionaries began arriving to evangelize the Maguindanao. Three different evangelical missions had joined forces in sending out more than a dozen teams of young couples, all well educated with keen minds and all highly trained in Islamics. It was a very promising company, some from far-flung continents of the world, lending an international flavor to the group. We looked forward to their using our translated Scriptures.

Sadly, by the time our four years in Cotabato had come to an end, all of these young missionaries had left for one reason or another, most of which involved physical and mental health. They seemed not to be prepared for spiritual warfare. Also, there was not the emphasis on prayer and humility, which characterized the missionaries working amongst the Maranaos. When the last couple left Cotabato, their contextualization of Muslim rituals and dress had been so extreme that the Muslim elders boasted that they had made converts of this young American couple. By the time Bob had completed the translation of the four Gospels as well as Genesis and Exodus in Maguindanao, there was not a single missionary left to use them.

Meanwhile, the missionaries in our former area, more of whom had been arriving in our absence, were eager to have the Old Testament translated into Maranao. Before we made the transfer back, however, my old nemesis, typhoid, struck again. As the fever peaked, we received a telegram from Fred, our missionary friend back in Iligan, telling of a house available for rent there. We didn't know we were looking for a house!

As for the unpublished Maguindanao Scriptures, we had the joy eleven years later of printing five hundred copies and delivering them in person to Tom, the new missionary in Cotabato, who immediately put them to good use in his fruitful ministry.

Chapter 11

The Maranao Old Testament

With no missionaries left in Cotabato, it was time to return to Lanao and the Maranao Old Testament. Still recovering from my second bout of typhoid, I joined Bob on unsteady legs for a three-day house-hunting trip to the town of Iligan on the north shore of Mindanao. It was next to the Maranao province, where Lake Lanao nestled high up on the mountaintop like a sparkling sapphire set against the emerald forest. Although Iligan was at the foot of this mountain and in close proximity to Muslim Lanao, it was nevertheless outside of Muslim control and boasted the comparative safety of a military garrison.

We boarded one of the last Philippine Airline flights to land at the Iligan airport, which, even by 1988, was already a very troubled area. The airport was halfway between Muslim and "Christian" territory, within easy range of Muslim fire. Aeronautically speaking, it was also a troubled area. Surrounding mountains created treacherous cross winds, which had taken out two passenger planes in the two previous months, leaving no survivors. This was our last move across the large island of Mindanao. We never left Iligan after that, although houses were sold out from under us several times.

Back to Maranao Translation

Bob's first project in Iligan was to translate Campus Crusade's *Jesus* film project, which he also directed while local missionaries brought in the Maranao voices for dubbing. More movies followed, including *The Bridge,* but these involved only the translation, not the directing, which was done in Manila.

Next, Bob tackled Psalms and Proverbs, fully expecting to complete them in three months. Instead, Psalms proved to be one of the most difficult books in the Bible to translate because of the ambiguity in the Hebrew text, which resulted in a plethora of possible meanings. As Bob depended on the Holy Spirit's help in deciding on each word to use, three months lengthened into three years before we were ready to take the two books to the printer in Manila.

During these years in Iligan, Bob perfected his recipe for cooking a palatable and nutritious loaf of the Bread of Life.

Bread of Life Recipe

Basic and essential ingredients:

Thorough knowledge of the target language, Maranao

Working knowledge of the source languages, Greek and Hebrew

The help of a variety of native speakers, some educated, some not

Mix ingredients together thoroughly with the following helps:

Original texts in Greek and Hebrew—interlinear if needed

Lexicons and commentaries on the original languages

Great variety of English translations, old and new

(good computer software will provide all of these helps)

To make it palatable and nutritious, fold in a very large quantity of:

Seasoning of prayer for the illumination of the

Holy Spirit (fringe benefit is enthusiasm and encouragement)

Pour thoroughly mixed ingredients into a good desktop publishing program and bake in hot oven for many hours of uninterrupted desk time

Yield:
photo-ready copy of Maranao Scriptures for the printer!

Bob has never been known for his culinary expertise. In fact, the Bread of Life is his only recipe, but he had many years of experience in perfecting it. Unlike all other recipes, however, it had the unique characteristic of being unpalatable without prayer!

With the Holy Spirit's help, Bob continued "baking" for twenty more years in Iligan, interrupted only by a prostatectomy, for which my brother Kway was his urologist. There followed a string of skin cancers, which proved to be an occupational hazard for both of us. Carcinoma robbed him of half an ear, but as the plastic surgeon cheerfully reassured us, "No one looks at both ears at the same time!"

We both had a series of melanomas to deal with, and when our two grown sons joined us with their own melanomas, we became somewhat of a dermatological wonder, with four in the same family afflicted. However, Greig was a Northwest pilot, and his passes enabled us to return to the States annually instead of staying on the field for four years at a stretch. This was indeed a timely blessing.

Immigration Status

The Peaceful Revolution took place in the mid eighties, when "People Power" ousted President Marcos without firing a shot and replaced the dictator with Cory Aquino, whose late husband had been felled by the Marcos regime. The new government lost no time in attempting to clean house. It embarked on the unlikely project of purging its ranks of graft and corruption, targeting first the Department of Immigration. This left missionaries with antiseptic burns—we were without valid visas!

Alien residents were required to appear before a judge who personally interviewed each one, and many were denied visa renewals, including some missionaries. It was the desire and goal of the Catholic Church to rid the country of Protestant missionaries, especially now that they had a devout Catholic in the presidency. After all, the Philippines was already a Christian country. Or was it?

We went up to Manila for our hearing and waited outside the courtroom at the Department of Immigration, listening to the trial of a German woman posing as a missionary but who had, in fact, been selling Filipino babies for adoption in Germany, a strictly illegal enterprise. The next was a Swedish man who had been smuggling weapons into the Philippines for Marcos loyalists. Hundreds of foreigners were expelled from the country during this period.

When our turn came we were ushered into the courtroom with both a defense and prosecuting lawyer. The questions being set forth, in one way or another, were: Why are missionaries still here in this already Christianized country? and, When can you wrap things up and leave? They were interested in how much social work a missionary was engaged in and how much money each foreigner could invest in the Philippines.

As Bob was called before the bench, the judge seemed especially interested in the voluminous stack of books he had brought in defense. It included translated Scriptures as well as published linguistic articles. When the trial was over, the judge apologetically thanked Bob for his time!

A whole year passed before we learned the outcome of our trial, which turned out to be, not only a renewed visa, but the coveted permanent resident visa. This meant we would not have to go up to Manila every year to renew our visas. In fact, we would never again have to renew them for as long as we wished to live in the Philippines. Favor! The work God had given us to do was not yet finished, and once again He had granted us His favor.

God Hides Us

Back in Lanao, Maranao threats to kill us were still very much alive. One time our phone rang and the voice on the other end asked, "Where are you located?" I hung up quickly and called the phone company to cut that line. It was the only telephone line that reached Marawi City, where the call had obviously originated. Another time Maranaos showed up at the local Visayan church we attended and asked where we lived. The staff wisely steered them in the opposite direction.

And so, we stayed hidden for many years until the entire Bible was translated and the dedication over. In the years which followed these first threats, the Lord hid us from the Lakeside Maranaos who intended to harm us, and to this day He has shielded Bob's numerous language assistants, in particular Tendug, the one who worked most closely with him for many years. The Holy Spirit has protected His Word, as well as those working to make it available.

Tendug

Tendug was by far the most colorful of all Bob's language assistants, as well as the one with the greatest longevity in the work. We met him in the sixties, shortly before the Blackshirt/Ilaga War. He arrived in Wao with his lovely Visayan wife, whom he had acquired while living in a distant coastal city. She was not prepared, however, for life in a pure Muslim barrio and was nearly paralyzed by fear, so it was not surprising to learn that she had taken their two little boys and fled to her parents' home on a far-off island. Knowing that he would never see his wife or sons again, Tendug accepted his loss with true Muslim fatalism.

"It is the will of Allah," he said with masked stoicism.

Later, when we returned from our Dallas sojourn in the seventies and made a trip back to Wao looking for a language assistant, we stayed overnight with Datu Tao. As we slept on the Datu's bed, Bob kept hearing the name "Tendug" going over in his mind like a broken record. In the morning he realized it was the Lord and shot out of bed to look for him.

"Today is my very last day of harvest," Tendug beamed, delighted to accept Bob's offer of work.

We had not really known Tendug before this, and it came as a joyful surprise to learn that he had been born and raised on the Lake, which meant his dialect was unadulterated by Wao colloquialism! Once again the Holy Spirit was guarding the purity of His Word for the densely populated Lake area.

For the next three years Tendug worked faithfully helping Bob revise the New Testament, but from the moment it was published, Tendug's life was never out of danger.

While we were in Dallas in the seventies, Tendug had acquired a Muslim wife, who by then had given him several children. Once when we returned to Wao after our month of work in the city, we found him walking on cloud nine. His wife had delivered their sixth child the night before, a strapping baby boy. His first child, although a boy, was a deaf mute, followed by four girls. Now he had a healthy boy, and to top it off, Tendug had performed the delivery himself!

Tendug's wife, Pemuki, was the barrio midwife, and the only other midwife was a forgetful old woman whose eyesight was failing. Tendug was not about to entrust her with this propitious event. In breach of Muslim taboos, he took charge of the delivery and postpartum care himself. His mother-in-law, with her two small children, was visiting from the Lake, but she stayed downstairs the whole time, not fancying night work. Tendug's excitement and joy over having another son buoyed him up during the sleepless nights and bleary-eyed days which followed.

By the time we moved into the comparative security of Iligan, Tendug had returned to his native Marawi City to seek his fortune. This, of course, was the Lord's doing, as it was only an hour's drive by public jeepney down the mountain from Marawi to our house in Iligan. He was happy to make the trip several days a week for the large salary Bob agreed to pay.

Keenly aware of the danger in which this work placed Tendug, I asked him one day what he told his neighbors when he left home in the morning.

"I tell them I am going to teach at the university in Iligan," he said with a sly grin. He had indeed attended college for a couple of years, but his neighbors did not realize that he could not teach anywhere without a degree.

By the mid-nineties, Tendug's burgeoning family had swelled to nine children, who generated tensions with their ongoing escapades. They ranged in age from two to twenty-five and kept life catapulting from crisis to emergency.

Boni, the deaf mute, was the oldest, and it had been weighing heavily on Tendug that his eldest son, who was handicapped, still had no wife after several attempts to secure one for him. So it was that Tendug and his wife, Pemuki, set off with their son to fetch him a bride. They went to Wao hoping it would be easier and less expensive to find a country girl from a remote farming community.

It is the boy's parents who are expected to take the initiative in locating a bride, and the biggest hurdle is negotiating an acceptable dowry. The more educated and lighter complexioned the girl, the higher the bride price. Tendug was looking for a dark-skinned, uneducated one, and he had in mind a former neighbor of ours. Since the negotiations hit a snag, however, he switched to a new family in the community, who also had a fifteen year old daughter. The young couple had never met, but that was no obstacle. Determined not to come home empty-handed, Tendug's five-day mission lengthened into ten before the knot was tied.

Limited as he is in communication skills, Boni was apprehensive of the ceremony itself. During a Maranao wedding, the *imam* holds the groom's hand and says, "Before almighty Allah, are you willing to accept this woman as your wife and pay the agreed upon dowry?" to which the groom responds, "Yes." Tendug had a prearranged signal with his son, that when the moment came in the ceremony for the groom to say yes, Tendug would nudge him inconspicuously. When he did this, Boni, who was born and raised among this crowd, astounded them all by nodding enthusiastically in the affirmative. They were amazed that deaf Boni would know when to respond, and Tendug was delighted with himself for having pulled it off.

It is strictly forbidden for a man to ever touch a Muslim girl until they are married, and in some Muslim weddings the bride does not even appear. Instead, the groom's friends and male relatives escort him to the house where the bride is waiting, and he touches her on the arm, thus signifying that they are now man and wife.

Since this bride was so young, Tendug wisely persuaded her mother to come back to Marawi with them to teach her daughter "how to be a wife." Culture demanded that the mother, for her part, have a companion for herself, so she brought two of her small children with her, and everyone squeezed into Tendug's tiny city house, along with his own nine children. There was one small room downstairs, which served as a visiting area, and an even smaller family bedroom at the top of the ladder.

The young bride entered her new environment with overwhelming shyness and fear, never having left home or family before. For a while Boni was the personification of thoughtfulness and became her knight in shining armor, preparing food for her, catering to her every need, and encouraging her to eat since she had developed an appetite problem. In short, he was courting his bride. With the passing of time, however, this got old, especially when the girl kept crawling in bed with his parents every night, which was not hard to do since everyone sleeps side by side on a thin mat on the floor. Her mother had returned to Wao by the end of the first week, and the young bride kept talking about going home, too, but Tendug persuaded her to stay.

Finally, the entire household could no longer deny the fact that something was seriously wrong with this latest addition to the family. The new wife was mentally unbalanced! As her bizarre behavior became increasingly obvious, Tendug called in the local shaman, whose greater demon was apparently able to subdue the girl's lower-level demons, temporarily at least. This was folk Islam at its best!

The girl's parents, of course, were well aware of their daughter's deficiency, which ran in the family, and not surprisingly with so much intermarriage between first cousins in Wao. Her family had been delighted to pawn her off on unsuspecting Tendug and collect the dowry. There was nothing left for him to do but return her to her family, especially since Boni could no longer stand the sight of her. Forfeiting the dowry was the most painful turn of events for Tendug.

Before the flaws in Boni's wife were identified, Tendug's second son, Orak, who was by then seventeen years old, was married under very different circumstances. His young sweetheart, who hailed from a prominent Marawi City family, was found to be pregnant, which is ample grounds for the death sentence for the couple. The only way Tendug could save his son's life, as well as his own, was to raise an enormous dowry and approach the girl's parents before they found out she was in the family way. Somehow, he was able to come up with the right amount in the nick of time. Had her parents suspected the awful truth, a dowry of even ten times that amount would not have been sufficient to prevent the father from taking the life of both Orak and Tendug.

The frosting on the cake came when the girl delivered her baby after just two months of marriage! Her unsuspecting parents were stunned, although even twins could easily have been lost in the folds of a Muslim woman's habit. The father was livid and reached for his gun. Fortunately, Tendug's wife, Pemuki, was the midwife on hand for the event. She had never been to school, but she had already logged in more deliveries than an American OB would in a lifetime! She jumped up, frantically interceding for her men, who fortunately were nowhere in the vicinity, and was able to calm the enraged grandfather with the news that the baby boy was a carbon copy of himself.

The hilarious denouement came when Orak complained to his father, "The baby is not handsome like me. He's very ugly. He looks just like my father-in-law!"

The Pendulum Swings

Over the years, Tendug continued to come down the mountain to work with Bob, entertaining us with the antics of his large family. Daily we prayed for his salvation as the pendulum swung between his professions of faith and his obvious allegiance to Islam. Did he or did he not know Jesus as his Savior and Lord?

When Bob invited him to watch the *Jesus* movie, Tendug asked if he could say the prayer that came at the end. Bob was elated. It was a prayer for salvation, where he asked Jesus to be the Lord of his life. On the other hand, we had to keep in mind that third world culture, unlike Western culture, does not favor independent decisions. Being in Bob's employ, furthermore, put Tendug under self-imposed pressure to please the one who paid his salary, which results in nothing more than a rice Christian.

After all those years of working with Bob, Tendug had a rather thorough knowledge of the Bible. Although he agreed enthusiastically with its message, it was not understanding which he lacked but rather a surrender of his life to the lordship of Christ. Fear, of course, was the primary factor in his not making a clean break with Islam, or any break at all, for that matter. Demonic bondage was also a powerful hindering force.

One day, in the midst of a conversation concerning eternal life, Tendug gave us reason to be encouraged. "My heart feels different inside since I have been working with you," he offered.

Again our hopes soared, and we rejoiced in answered prayer for Tendug's salvation. Until, that is, it became obvious that he considered himself a Muslim in good standing, in short, a devout follower of Muhammad. His faithful attendance at the mosque every Friday as well as his strict adherence to the fast of Ramadan dispelled our hopes, as he continued to put forth every effort to earn his salvation from Allah.

"Will you please tell me again what are the differences between the Muslim and Christian way of salvation?" Tendug said one day.

The pendulum had swung again, and with it our expectations rose, only to be dashed once more. There was no real change of heart or mind. Someone has said that a Muslim must hear the gospel one hundred times before he can understand and accept it. Tendug must have heard the gospel a thousand times as he worked with Bob, and yet hearing it generated no apparent change in his life. Muslims who come to the Lord through dreams and visions, on the other hand, make the break with Muhammad quickly. How could they do otherwise after a personal encounter with the Lord?

Tendug took his life in his hands every time he came down the mountain to work with Bob, which was an hour's journey from Muslim Marawi City. One day he left for greener pastures. The provincial governor had a building project in a distant area and had not been able to get a foreman he could trust with either money or personnel until a relative of his discovered Tendug. The remuneration was vastly greater than Bob could ever pay him. This possibility had hung like a shroud over our horizon for a number of years, and at last we had to say with Job, "That which I feared has come upon me!"

After working with Bob for more than thirty years, Tendug was invaluable, as every word had to be checked by a native speaker. We worried about a replacement, but God in His faithfulness always supplied that need and never left Bob without the necessary help.

Demon Pebbles

When our second house in Iligan was sold out from under

us, we moved one final time, but once again we failed to cleanse the house immediately. Instead, we fell wearily into bed our first night there, only to regret our procrastination. Just as we were dropping off to sleep, we heard strange noises from outside as though someone were throwing tiny pebbles at our window. They were not hard enough to break the glass, but disturbing enough to rob us of sleep. We had heard that the neighbors were friendly, but now their children didn't seem to be very well behaved. Each time we got up to investigate, however, there was perfect silence from outside, and the neighbors, whose bedrooms we could look right into, were fast asleep. Furthermore, our whole house seemed to be creaking, as though someone were trying to break in. We should have known better by this time, but we were exhausted after a long, hard day of packing, loading, and unloading the truck. We were too tired to think.

When we woke up unrefreshed the next morning, Bob announced, "The activity last night was demonic." Of course! How could we have missed it? We had done ourselves a disfavor by not cleansing the entire house and surroundings before trying to sleep. We lost no time in doing just that, and that was the end of the demon pebbles.

In the house before that it was an army of rats that thundered across the house at night in the space between the ceiling and roof. They, too, left when Satan was bound. Knowing that her house had been haunted, the landlady asked me one day to give her the formula we had used to rid her house of spirits. I explained that a ritual would not work, a fact she knew only too well, having paid large sums of money to more than one priest and shaman for that purpose. Exorcism, I told her, could only be done through the Holy Spirit's power by someone who was a friend of God, all of which took much explaining.

Animism is so deeply rooted in Philippine culture that the people are spirit-sensitive. Demons are recognized and accepted as part of life but always feared. Since no one wants to share his home with ghosts if he can avoid it, frequently haunted houses have provided us with inexpensive rent. Our intrigued neighbors have often asked the question as to what ritual we had used to rid the house of spirits, and this has afforded rich opportunities over the years to explain that it's not a formula but a Person, and that Person is far more powerful than the unholy spirits in the house. At times they have concluded that white-skinned people are not bothered by demons. Far from it! We have witnessed more than one missionary casualty as a result of not recognizing the source of their problem.

The powers of darkness are a poignant reminder of our responsibility in the area of spiritual warfare and of the devourer who is always on the prowl. It is the same devourer who blinds Muslim hearts. On the other hand, we reveled in the glorious angels assigned to watch over God's people.

By the year 2000, the military had made strategic gains over Muslim rebels. Nevertheless, although the rebels abandoned their stronghold, there was no surrender, and their leader, Nur Misuari, managed to slip out of the country. From his cushy vantage point in exile, he continued to hold command, calling for jihad. Against this backdrop of ongoing conflict, however, the government attempted to hold peace talks with Misuari, who claimed that the only way peace would ever come to Mindanao was for the entire island to be under the "protection" of his army, the MNLF (Moro National Liberation Front). The MNLF, however, was little more than a collection of Muslim bandits armed by Middle Eastern terrorists. No lasting progress has ever been made on the island of Mindanao.

Chapter 12

The Brave Team of Visayan Evangelists

Shortly after we returned to Iligan, we had an unexpected visit from a group of Christian college students from Marawi City. We were back in Lanao, on the fringe of Maranao territory, and Marawi was only an hour's jeepney ride up the mountain from us. The students were Visayan believers studying at the government university there who had united under the banner of "Household of Faith." Their purpose was to evangelize Muslims in the dangerous city of Marawi. Hearing that the translator for the Maranao Bible was living in Iligan, they came down the mountain to find us, and what a day we had! It was a thrilling surprise to discover there were Filipino believers with the same mandate as ours. We were a mutual encouragement to each other that day, as we were many days in the years which followed. They returned to campus that evening carrying a heavy load of Maranao Scriptures.

Saturday R & Rs

From then on we became dad and mom to this brave team. About a dozen students came regularly on the first Saturday of each month to spend their day off with us. They would arrive bursting with excitement over the latest harrowing event and bubbling with news of open doors. They came to relax and unwind and to seek encouragement, counsel, and direction. It was a time for them to regroup, a time to step back and gain a higher perspective. Without realizing it, they were conducting a mini seminar every month.

Much of the day was spent in eating as we pampered them with every delicacy available, especially meat, which was in scarce supply in Marawi and which slim wallets could ill afford. After a sumptuous noon meal topped off with enormous servings of ice cream and after hashing over the latest crisis, we would spend the rest of the afternoon praying and singing together. Reinvigorated by the Holy Spirit, they would leave as evening shadows stole across the sky.

One day the group decided the Lord wanted them to stage a Jericho march in Marawi City on Easter Sunday morning. This bordered on suicide in that fanatically Islamic town, but their leader, Ghenie, went boldly to the mayor of Marawi to request the necessary permission.

In his best politician's manner, the mayor responded affably, "Of course you can have your march. This is an open city." He was referring to the only closed city in the Philippines!

As Ghenie's jaw dropped and his eyes bulged in disbelief, the mayor added, "This town needs Jesus." He was mimicking Protestant lingo, of course, which was good PR, and to top it off, he assigned a military escort, a necessity in that hostile environment.

And so, the march was on. At 4 a.m. that Easter Sunday morning a large group of Visayan young people began their walk around Marawi City, carrying placards and waving slogans proclaiming, "Jesus is Lord," "Jesus is Savior," "Jesus is the only Way," and so forth. Every time they came to a place where there had been a recent killing, for which the town was noted, the marchers stopped and prayed, binding the demon spirits which rule Marawi City. At times their praying turned to "other tongues," and one time Maranao *ustads* (religious teachers) standing nearby recognized the Arabic language being clearly articulated by three of these Visayan young people, none of whom had ever heard a word of Arabic in their lives!

Incredibly, instead of a backlash, the feedback that reached them was favorable. Impressed by the clean-cut lives of the students, several young Muslims visited their services from time to time, joining in the lively singing. The group flourished, staking a claim for a Maranao church in the kingdom of God. Theirs was the stuff of martyrs, and indeed, three of them came close to being just that in the years that followed.

Before we met these students, seven young Maranaos had been born again and baptized in the waters of Lake Lanao! All seven, however, disappeared soon afterward, without leaving a trace. It was believed that they were alive, but that each one had suddenly been forced to flee for his life. Two were seen later in Iligan, though only briefly in passing, while the others escaped to Manila.

Eventually the team moved out of the comfort and security of the university campus into the heart of the city, where they rented a couple of rooms in a dilapidated lodging house, which they affectionately dubbed "The Mission House." There, in the very heart of Muslim Marawi City, they conducted a one-on-one ministry to Maranao young people, witnessing in the secrecy of their rooms. They brought Maranaos there at all times of the day and night to hold in-depth Bible studies and to discuss Christian apologetics.

Christmas

On Christmas Day the team arrived in Iligan to enjoy the festivities with us. The main dish for our feast was a large fish, complete with head and tail, along with roast pork, an unheard of treat for Christians living in a Muslim community. There were other Asian dishes, of course, always with an emphasis on meat. After the meal, we shared Scriptures the Lord had given us for each of the young people. And we sang—how they could sing! And we prayed—how they could pray, storming the gates of heaven where God smiled on them. There were more native delicacies before our merry good-byes. Nearly all of them were far from home, and this was the only Christmas celebration any of them would have. It was among our happiest in the Philippines.

Sad to say, Ghenie fell into a life of immorality, and like Judas, he was stealing from the team's purse, leaving the others in Marawi without food while he dissipated time and money in the gay community of Iligan. Tragically, an unrepentant Ghenie left the team, never to return. He sailed off to another island, where he was brutally murdered the following year.

Kidnapped

Returning from the post office one day, I was greeted at the door by a somber-faced husband. "The boys have been kidnapped!" Bob said gravely.

I slumped into a chair in the living room, where the girls from the team were waiting, still breathless, to tell the whole story all over again. One of the girls was Letty, the sister of Laloy, who had been kidnapped. Late in the afternoon on the day before while the girls were away, three boys who were left in the Mission House were invited to a Maranao wedding. Clueless, they stepped outside into a waiting jeepney, only to find themselves in the hands of kidnappers. Sadly, it was Mohaiman, one of their early converts, who betrayed them by luring them into the trap. He had lived in the Mission House for several months while being discipled, but now he could not resist the temptation of money as well as an opportunity to be restored to the good graces of his Muslim peers.

Later that evening, Mohaiman returned to get the unsuspecting girls, bearing with him a note from Laloy. The kidnappers had forced Laloy to write the note urging the girls to join them at the wedding, but it was not hard for the girls to read between the lines and decipher the coded warning. He used several difficult and obscure Visayan words that the Maranao kidnappers could not understand. Mercifully, the Lord intervened as the girls huddled in prayer. One of them had been in slight physical discomfort and they pled sick. Quickly they nailed the wooden windows shut and waited out the night, fleeing before dawn on the first jeepney headed for Iligan.

Three days later we received a phone call from "our friendly kidnappers," as we nicknamed them. They had come down to Iligan to phone, because Marawi as yet had no telephone contact with the outside world. They demanded that we pay an enormous ransom and turn over Ghenie, who was long gone by this time. Missionaries, of course, have an unwritten understanding that no ransom is ever paid. Otherwise the others would all be sitting ducks.

After soliciting prayer from every church in Iligan and after phoning the States, where our daughter Carole added the crisis to a string of prayer chains, we stopped to pray ourselves. Meanwhile news of the boys' plight soon spread throughout the entire world. Next we enlisted the help of a new secret Maranao believer named Omar. Several days later, a mail delivery service brought us a tape and letters from the boys, obviously recorded under duress.

Nevertheless, we were confident that the boys would be released soon. I replenished our supply of rice and stocked the fridge with fat chickens and liter-size Cokes against the day when they would walk smilingly into our house and a celebration would be in order. The weeks dragged on, however, bringing no encouraging news. The Cokes dwindled and the chickens disappeared as the remaining members of the team dropped by day after day to exchange rumors and be updated, but mostly to pray desperately for the safety and release of their teammates.

Being Maranao, Omar was able to make radio contact with the kidnappers, which revealed by the position on the radio dial the general area the boys were being held. They were in the mountains at the far end of Lake Lanao, thirty kilometers from Marawi City. Other than that, we were back to square one with no apparent progress having been made after weeks of prayerful suspense.

We never knew when the kidnappers, frustrated by not being able to collect a ransom, would renew their attempts to pick up the other members of the team. Consequently, we urged them all to return to their homes in the distant corners of our island of Mindanao, which they did. Meanwhile, the boys' lives hung precariously in the balance.

It is the custom of Muslim kidnappers to pass their victims along to another group of rebels every couple of weeks, thus sharing the spoils as well as the risk of being apprehended. Maranaos, more than the other Muslim tribes, however, have the reputation of killing their victims early on if their demands are not met quickly. It was easier to kill their victims than to keep passing them along with no hope of reward. But the Lord was hearing prayer and kept this from happening. In light of the fact that these were all poor boys from families who could never pay a ransom, it became obvious that their angels were watching closely over them.

Hit and Run Trips to Marawi

These were stressful days for us, too, as we drove several times a week to forbidden Marawi City to appeal to the governor or his wife, Princess Johaira, who was running for mayor; to Princess Tarhata, the former governor; the very powerful Assemblyman Bolindong; and others. On our first trip we made it back only by the grace of God. Consequently, we had the windows of our SUV tinted with the darkest shade available, hoping this would provide protection along the way, while we disguised ourselves. On one occasion, a compassionate mayor's wife was horrified at seeing white faces in Marawi and insisted on sending an armed escort back to Iligan with us. She didn't think much of our disguise. These trips availed nothing, however, except to give us the satisfaction that we had done everything we could.

As weeks lengthened into months, news leaked out that the boys had been transferred to the neighboring province of Cotabato into the hands of Maguindanao rebels. This was good news, as Maguindanaos were more Westernized and not as cruel as the other two major Muslim groups.

With great fortitude, the mothers of two of the boys

ventured off to Cotabato to look for their sons, whom they eventually found on a tiny island, and returned to give us a report. From the women we learned that for the first three weeks in captivity, the boys were hog-tied and starved, but in keeping with the modus operandi, they were passed from captor to captor until they ended up in the hands of the more humane Maguindanaos. Mike however, who was tall, was ghostly thin by that time. The mothers soon went back to "Kidnap Island" and refused to leave without their sons!

During their earlier ordeal at the hands of Maranaos, the boys were continually threatened. Once when the guard issued the order, "Say your last prayer before we kill you," deep emotions surfaced, and the three boys raised loud voices to heaven. Mike, the youngest, told the Lord he was very ready to die and go to be with Jesus. Manolo, the eldest and the spiritual father of the team, cried out to the Lord, begging Him for more time to serve Him. Laloy protested in dismay, "But Lord, I thought I would be here when You returned." He very well may be!

Six weeks had gone by after they disappeared, and it was in the best interest of the boys and their families for us to remove ourselves from the scene before further demands prolonged their ordeal. Moreover, the military had received intelligence that we were next on the list. We slipped hurriedly away from the island of Mindanao, but not before contacting Sister Emma, a pastor friend with whom we left money and instructions for the boys to travel to Manila as soon as they were released to attend a short-term Bible school. We felt it would be therapeutic for them to get as far away from our island as possible to facilitate their emotional healing as well as to give them the much-coveted opportunity of Bible training. It did, indeed, accomplish both goals.

Shortly after we arrived home in Dallas, we received a phone call from Willi, one of the Iligan missionaries. The local police chief had "definite information" that we had been kidnapped, and Willi promised to check this out.

The long-awaited news of the boys' release finally arrived on Easter Sunday. A pastor on Mindanao phoned Dallas to tell us that the boys had just arrived at his church. God, in answer to the prayers of the church worldwide, effected that release. This called for the greatest celebration ever, and indeed the boys were doing just that. After three long months and many episodes in captivity, they were free to tell tales, and they had many tales to tell. No money had been paid, and it was a miracle that they had not been killed before the first month was out.

Although the boys had been tied and starved for the first three weeks and were often threatened with execution, it was the remaining months with the amazing answers to prayer which they remembered best. Commander Jun, one of the rebels in charge of the operation, became convinced by their bold witness that Jesus is God, and one day, before going out on a sortie, he asked the boys to pray for his safety. When he returned, he rewarded them with a surprise—an English Bible!

Another time, when the boys were allowed to go down to the river to bathe, they gave a powerful witness for Jesus to their guard, who immediately came under deep conviction of sin and sobbed convulsively as the boys led him to faith in Christ!

The *imams* had been demanding that we turn over our entire supply of Maranao Scriptures, which we refused to do out of respect for the Iligan pastors, who asked us not to. "If we give in to the demands of the Muslims now, where will this end?" the pastors reasoned, and we submitted to their counsel.

Because of these demands, a friend of the boys went to their Marawi City lodgings and brought the entire remaining supply of Maranao Scriptures, half a rice sack full, and surrendered them as a peace offering to the kidnappers. Instead of burning them, however, as per the instruction of the *ustads* and *ulamas*, the rebels made a dash for the sack, each one grabbing a hard-bound New Testament and running off with it until there was nothing left to burn. What an example of God's unique method of Scripture distribution!

The best part came when the angry *imams* told the kidnapped boys, "You do not know how many of our Maranao young people have turned away from Islam as a result of the Christian holy book you have been circulating! We do not care if you distribute the Bible in English or any Filipino dialect, but *not* in our Maranao language!" It's the Word in one's mother tongue that reaches the heart!

There was no reason for the boys to have been released, except God. They were free in time to spend several weeks with their families before boarding the inter-island ferry for the two-day voyage to Manila, where they attended YWAM's Discipleship Training School. It was the very first time any of them had been off the island of Mindanao, and the six months of training proved to be a dream realized for all of them. The Lord had wonderfully answered the prayers of the body of Christ worldwide.

Omar

The year 1992 was an eventful one indeed. The calendar was taken up with kidnappings and weddings. Shortly after the three boys were released, Sharon, our youngest, married Cleve, a young deacon from our church in Dallas. When we returned to the Philippines, another wedding soon followed when Omar, a secret Maranao believer with an intriguing story, wed Laloy's sister, Letty. He was a brilliant young intellectual whose first novel had recently been published in Manila.

Omar was not won to Christ through human witness or persuasion. He was an intellectual who came to the Lord "through grace," as he quaintly explained. Like the apostle Paul's experience, Jesus appeared to Omar in a vision. While still a Muslim, he had been inducted into the elite corps of the Coalition of Islamic Movements in Marawi City. He was also the spokesman for the Islamic Brotherhood, one of the most extreme fundamentalist Islamic organizations in the world. He hailed from a prominent family and was a high profile member of the Hezbollah. Initially, he resisted the implications of the vision, but later repented and considered it his most heinous sin.

While still refusing to embrace the vision, Omar stumbled into a Pentecostal church on an unrelated errand. Out of courtesy to the pastor, whose participation in dialogue he was soliciting, Omar stayed for the full service. It was during the worship time while the congregation was singing "Worthy" that the Holy Spirit moved deeply in his heart, and he could no longer deny that the Jesus who had appeared to him in vision was indeed God. Being filled with fear of the consequences, however, he kept this conviction to himself.

Later, Omar decided it would be better to entrust his life to Jesus than to live a life of fear. With renewed zeal and enlarged vision, he became incredibly bold until he, along with a handful of fellow secret believers, was discovered. He was apprehended by his Muslim peers, and his life hung by a thread as he was brought before an Islamic tribunal on the university campus in Marawi. The president of the college at that time happened to be his first cousin, who issued the ultimatum, "Give up Christianity if you wish to live." Attempts to carry out that threat soon materialized.

When we returned from the States after Cleve and Sharon's wedding, Omar and Letty came to tell us of their plans to marry and to ask for our blessing. In sharp contrast to the beautiful wedding in Dallas, the venue of this one was changed several times, right up to the night before, while Omar was being hunted down by Muslim extremists. Finally, with a handful of close friends around them, they exchanged vows in a tiny Methodist church at the end of a remote alley in Iligan. There was not much tradition and few dry eyes, but the Lord was there.

We sent them off for a three-day honeymoon at the beach, but unfortunately their wedded bliss ended abruptly as their marriage turned into a series of narrow escapes from would-be assassins. Word of Omar's defection had leaked to the Maranao chapter of Hezbollah, of which he had been a leader, and they were hot on his trail. Three times in the next few weeks Omar was nearly killed by various members of the Hezbollah, including his own brothers whose responsibility it was to purge the family name.

No sooner had Omar and Letty returned to Marawi after their honeymoon than Omar was given three days to renounce his Christian faith or die. When threats failed to accomplish anything more than terrify him, his tormentors began two weeks of intense interrogations. The Hezbollah decided it would be bad press to make a martyr out of a brilliant intellectual from a prominent family who had just published his first novel. So they focused their efforts on trying to force him to renounce his apostasy and return to the fold of Islam. It was an all-out effort to break him, hence the round-the-clock interrogations which left him at the breaking point physically, mentally, and emotionally. Quite a way to start a marriage!

"*Ate* Mariel, I am so exhausted! I just don't know what to do," came Omar's cry for help ringing over the telephone. This was after two intense weeks of brainwashing during which Omar was taken to the mosque at all hours of the day and night for endless questioning. He slipped away from watchful eyes for a moment into an obscure phone booth, so worn out he could hardly talk.

Sensing that he would have to hang up any second, I shot back, "Read Psalm 91 and remember, Omar, Christians are praying for you."

It was the prayers of the church that bore Omar up, and it was these prayers which miraculously drew aside the curtain of hate and torment for one evening while Omar seized the opportunity to give his complete, unabridged testimony before the Hezbollah of how Jesus had appeared to him in a vision and proved beyond doubt that He was, indeed, God. Every member listed intently. This was the day following his urgent phone call!

The sessions at the mosque continued for a time after that, but less frequently. Then, for the second time, a plot to kill Omar nearly succeeded. In both instances his older brother was involved. Omar received a message one evening to go to his brother's house, but before leaving he warned Letty, "If I don't return, don't come looking for me." Letty's life had also been threatened if she didn't convert to Islam, and Omar worried about her.

There were six members of the Hezbollah waiting for him when he arrived at his brother's house that evening. Pointing a gun at him, one of them said to Omar's brother, "If you don't, I will." This led to an argument.

"Run," a voice whispered from behind, although to this day Omar does not know whose voice it was nor where it came from! He slipped away and jumped into a passing jeepney, yelling to the driver to step on it.

Omar enjoyed a brief respite after that, and he and Letty spent the following Saturday with us, unwinding. His taut nerves had been ready to snap, but the gloom of night gave way to the hope of early dawn. Tensions were released and Omar, understandably, was on a high and letting off steam. We ate and we laughed and we prayed together. It was good to see them both so relaxed.

In an about-face, Omar's cousin, president of the university in Marawi City, appointed Omar as chairman of the newly organized but short-lived Muslim/Christian Relations group which Philippine President Ramos had created the month before. Although the job offered a substantial salary, more important to the visionary Omar was the unlimited opportunity to bring peace to a beleaguered Mindanao. Furthermore, his brother, the one assigned to kill him, put out the welcome mat. He and his wife wanted to get better acquainted with Letty and see more of them. His former "brothers" of the Hezbollah, who two weeks earlier were ready to torture and shoot him, were now more than conciliatory, offering friendship and cooperation. Marawi held a bright future for Omar, and he was relishing life.

But we were troubled. Storm clouds were gathering, and our fears for Omar were realized. Having failed to break him by threats and then brainwashing, his enemies began a third, more deadly tactic, that of wooing him back to the fold. The devil's "love," however, is short-lived and plastic. Letty warned him not to trust the Hezbollah, but it was tempting now that his terrifying ordeal was over. When his physical life was in danger, the situation was grave, but when his soul was under attack, how grave the danger! It was not long, however, before even Omar saw through the new tactic.

A truly bright gleam in this dark picture were the pockets of Maranao believers Omar was able to unearth, believers no outsider had ever before heard about. Thirty here, twenty there, fifty in another place—all underground. One group, in far off Tagoloan, had written their own worship songs in Maranao, while Maranao Scriptures grew legs, penetrating the dark corners around the Lake.

With ominous warnings, it soon became obvious to Omar and Letty that if they wanted to stay alive, they would have to leave Mindanao immediately. They fled to Manila to lose themselves in the bustling crowds, where they have remained ever since. They tried for a while to find work in the Middle East, but each door kept closing at the last minute until they were finally forced to recognize the Lord's hand.

At one point, worn out by fear, frustration and discouragement, Omar actually made plans to return to the fold of Islam. Pausing on his way to the mosque, however, he was given another vision. He saw multitudes of Muslims entering a mosque, and he was made to know that all of them were headed for hell. Overcome by horror, he returned in repentance to Christ.

Omar's life was to remain bound by fear for several more years until the Lord broke that chain. He had a stepbrother living in Manila whom he had been afraid to visit or to speak a word to about his conversion. But one day a pastor friend in Manila challenged Omar.

"You go home and pray tonight, and I will do the same. Then tomorrow go to your brother."

Omar did exactly that and was so eager the next morning to share his faith with his brother that he left home at six o'clock in the morning and spent the rest of the day in bold witness to the saving work of Christ on the cross. As he stepped out onto the water, he was instantly and permanently delivered from fear. A new Omar, no longer consumed by the possibility that someone might be following him, had found peace at last. Conversion may take a moment, but discipleship, a lifetime.

What became of the team? They all married and entered Christian ministry in various parts of the Philippines, but, understandably, not on the island of Mindanao. Manolo and his American wife serve in the islands with YWAM, while Laloy ministers in Manila, where he keeps in touch with his sister Letty and her husband, Omar, and with us. Omar, for his part is engaged in educating Filipino young people in Islamics, preparing them to reach Muslims for Christ.

Chapter 13

A Year of Milestones and Celebrations

The Book of Job

When Bob began his translation of the Old Testament, he started with Psalms and was amazed at how challenging it was, having to decide on the exact Maranao word for every Hebrew concept. Not realizing it, however, he had actually left the most difficult book for last. When he began work on Job, he discovered that Psalms had merely provided training for Job, which is even more ambiguous in the Hebrew. He relished the challenge, however, and enjoyed working on Job more than on any other Scripture he had ever translated.

Though fascinating to translate, Job is often cryptic and written with unusual grammatical constructions, making use of a large number of very rare Hebrew words. While Psalms has many options for each Hebrew word, Job has more. A typical example of an unclear Hebrew text is Job 19:25–27. Hebrew scholars who first translated the Old Testament into Greek a couple of centuries before Christ came up with the following rendering which Bob then translated into English:

> For I know that he is eternal who is about to deliver me and to raise up upon the earth my skin that endures these sufferings: for these things have been accomplished to me of the Lord, which I am conscious of in myself.

Modern translations are hardly recognizable as the same verse, and even the four hundred year-old King James Version is a study in contrast:

> For I know that my Redeemer liveth, and that he shall stand at the latter day upon the earth: And though after my skin worms destroy this body, yet in my flesh shall I see God: Whom I shall see for myself.

Either rendering is possible from the Hebrew, but what a difference there is in the concepts conveyed to the reader. Without an abundant supply of the Holy Spirit's illumination, the translator is unable to adequately communicate the vital truths about God contained in a book like Job. It is only the Holy Spirit Himself, the author of the book, who can provide just the right word to make the text meaningful and, therefore, profitable to anyone, especially the Maranao, steeped as he is from birth in the teachings of Islam.

Physical Challenges

The year 2002 was one of physical challenges. For me Dengue Fever was a minor wrinkle along the way, followed close on its heels by surgery for the extraction of a tubercular tumor from my gums. This called for a TB regimen, which put considerable strain on an aging liver. Philippine doctors excel in treating TB because of the enormous amount of experience they have with it. On the other hand, they have very little opportunity to practice geriatrics, because few people in the third world live that long. Doctors in Manila expressed surprise at my having an oral tumor without ever having had TB of the lungs, but this was not hard for us to understand since I had high exposure to TB in the sixties, when I treated numerous advanced cases. It had lain dormant in my system for forty years.

No sooner was the TB under control than we were off to the island of Cebu for surgery on Bob's hand. No dermatologist would touch skin cancer at the base of his finger, where tendons were involved. The fast-growing lump had been excised before, but carcinoma had returned, this time with a vengeance. It was alarmingly reminiscent of several years earlier when he lost half an ear to skin cancer. Since he didn't have half a finger to spare, especially on his right hand, we went to the one and only orthopedic oncologist on our side of Manila. She was young, inexperienced, and ambitious, but God overruled her grandiose plans, and the end result was a smooth incision, beautifully repaired.

The First Celebration

The year 2005 was one of celebrations. Bob turned 80 in March, and that called for a trip home. We returned to Dallas for a delightful month of partying with friends and family, which had now grown to include fourteen grandchildren. That restful month was a good thing in light of our trip back to the Philippines, which turned out to be a nightmare. Somehow, we thought we could slide smoothly into home base. We thought it would be a breeze to wrap up the last phase of the work. Not so!

By then, all our trips were courtesy of Greig's Northwest passes. Although we were profoundly grateful for them and enjoyed the luxury of first class travel, it meant we were standbys, flying space-available. Before leaving the States, we stopped off to visit Bob's brother in Seattle, where Bob relished the nostalgia of reminiscing at his old childhood haunts. Seattle, however, was reluctant to let go of us! Without confirmed seats, we were bumped on flight after flight, day after day, for a whole week in the Seattle airport. Bone weary, we finally got the last two seats on a flight back to Manila, profoundly relieved to be on our way back even though our seats were not together. We had never been so happy to set foot on Philippine soil again.

The Largest Stone

The end was now in sight, and Bob was preparing a photo-ready copy of the entire Maranao Bible for printing in Manila. The Philippine Bible Society was the only organization in the country authorized to import Bible paper, which came from Japan, and we were grateful that they were handling that end of things. Meanwhile, the local missionaries were raising funds to pay for it.

Aware that the title for the Maranao Bible would be the widely used, official name for many decades to come, even as *Kitab Indil* (the New Testament) had been ever since it was published twenty-five years earlier, we asked workers to consider a name prayerfully, which they did. The Lord gave the title *So Sindaw* to a Maranao believer. It means "the Light"—not the light of a lamp or candle, but rather the all-encompassing, penetrating Light, the Light that came into the world and shines in the darkness.

Before the year was out, we sailed off to Manila with Bob's precious manuscript tucked securely under his arm. The Bible Society printed five thousand copies, while a few months later another mission printed six thousand more. In a year of milestones, some of the miles had been long, but this was the largest stone!

Just before taking the manuscript to Manila, we learned that Bob's PSA had risen significantly. Eighteen years after his prostatectomy, cancer had reared its ugly head again, indicating the need for a further procedure. While printing was in progress in Manila, we returned to Dallas for this surgery, using the time as well to buy a mobile home, where we would relocate in the States.

Golden Anniversary

Somewhere in this year of milestones and celebrations we found the time to celebrate our golden wedding anniversary with six golden days by the ocean in Davao on the eastern coast of Mindanao. Insulated by the gentle, untroubled waters of the Philippine Sea, where islands decorate the horizon and serenity stills the soul, we savored the loveliness of God's creation and reminisced on fifty years of the Lord's goodness and faithfulness. Davao was where we had spent our R & Rs in the eighties when we lived in Cotabato, so this was also closure for us, as well as our golden anniversary.

A Clandestine Dedication

Our third celebration was the most significant one of that eventful year, the dedication of the Maranao Bible, which actually spilled over into January of the following year. It made history. It was the first dedication of an entire Bible for Muslims in the last couple of centuries. We had nothing to do with planning the event itself, which was all done by the Iligan missionaries, who outdid themselves. Not in our wildest imagination could we picture what a Bible dedication for a Muslim ethnic group should be like, but the Lord gave them the creativity and energy to put together the most appropriate, God-honoring ceremony imaginable.

It was in sharp contrast to animistic tribes and their barrio-fiesta type of dedications. Almost without exception, these have been for the New Testament rather than a complete Bible, and have been large, public, open-air affairs with the butchering of a pig—enough to send chills down a Muslim spine. The Maranao dedication, on the other hand, was secretive to the point of being underground. It took place indoors, in the local church we had attended for many years, with only the pastor and head elder invited from the church. It was in the late afternoon while evening shadows stole across the sky, shrouding the event in obscurity.

The other guests were missionaries working with Maranaos, as well as Bible translators from various tribal groups on our island of Mindanao. The featured guests, however, were the Maranao believers, who shared their moving testimonies of how and why they had put their faith in Jesus Christ. There was nary a dry eye!

Never before had we seen so many Maranao believers in one place. It was the first gathering of its kind, bringing converts together from different parts of Mindanao, all followers of Jesus who never suspected there were so many other Muslims who had also put their trust in Christ. What an encouragement it was to each of them as well as to ourselves. The whole program honored the Lord and was carried out in such good taste, capturing the essence of what it was all about. The Lord was pleased, and we were overwhelmed.

Since then, *So Sindaw* has grown legs. As traveling merchants, Maranaos have penetrated the farthest corners of the islands, and the farther away they get from home, the safer they feel in exploring the Christian Bible.

After forty-five years of Bible translation in the Philippines, we turned our house keys over to our Iligan landlady and drove off with a missionary friend to the airport in the next province. It was February, 2006. As we made our way to Manila and on to Dallas, memories of God's faithfulness flooded our hearts and minds. In all those years He had never once failed us or broken a promise.

Chapter 14

Six Incredible Days on the Lake

The Challenge

"What would you attempt for God if you knew you couldn't fail?"

Jamie Buckingham, a prolific writer, died in 1992, but his words live on. When I read this challenge at the turn of the century, I didn't have to think. My answer came like a reflex. "I'd go to the Lake," I thought. But that was out of the question, of course. Evangelizing on Lake Lanao was a thing of the past. Even a brief visit was unthinkable by that time.

Tugaya, our first home in the Philippines, was two-thirds of the way down this ten-mile-long body of water. The sultan had adopted us as his son and daughter, and the Muslim barrio warmly welcomed our family. We were welcome, that is, until it became obvious that Bible translation was our purpose for being there. But even when they drove us out, there was a modicum of civility. They didn't terrorize us. We just knew we were no longer welcome and would never be able to get language assistants in that area.

The following decade saw Islamic fundamentalists pouring in from the Middle East, teaching Maranaos that the Jew was their eternal enemy and that the American was the friend of the Jew—teaching them, in short, to hate non-Muslims. Maranaos had never even heard the word *Jew* before that. By 1978 they were responsible for the first Christian martyr in Lanao, and kidnapping was gaining in popularity as a quick and easy way to get cash. Moreover, Muslims were getting away with it.

By the nineties it was extremely dangerous for outsiders to make even a hit-and-run trip into the provincial capital of Marawi City. We did slip in a number of times in our attempt to secure the release of the kidnapped boys, but our efforts availed nothing. By the turn of the century when I came across Jamie Buckingham's question, the Lake had long been off-limits for all non-Muslims, especially whites. Although I shrugged off Buckingham's challenge as impossible, I scribbled the words on a slip of paper and tucked their message away in the recesses of my mind where they etched themselves indelibly upon my subconscious.

Our daughter Carole, by then a missionary in Uganda, urged us to read Bill Johnson's book *When Heaven Invades Earth*. We bought it on our next trip to the States, but it sat untouched on our Iligan bookshelf while we were caught up in closure. By 2006 we had relocated to the States and were living in a Dallas suburb near our two younger children and their families. As soon as our barrels were unpacked, I picked up Johnson's book and couldn't put it down as I read about the power of God in healings and the gift of the word of knowledge.

"This is it," I kept saying to Bob. "This is how we can go to the Lake."

When Bob read the book, he agreed that the healing power of Jesus would open Muslim doors for us around the Lake. Miracle healings were not hard for us to have faith for after having seen the Lord heal one hundred percent of the people we prayed for in Wao. That was in '66, right after we received the Holy Spirit's baptism. All of them were terminal cases whom the local doctor had predicted would be dead by morning if they didn't receive surgery that day. We knew God would do the same again. After all, He's the same yesterday, today, and forever.

Back to the Lake

As we submitted this venture to the Lord, He gave us His peace and a green light to go. We boarded our Northwest flight that October with an urgency to carry out the task assigned us quickly before night fell and all work came to an end.

Bob had prepared a tract made up of Maranao verses in diglot. Half of each page was in Roman script and the other half in the Arabic script. Since all Maranaos on the Lake are taught from early childhood to sound out the Arabic letters, there would be no illiterates. The little tract clearly presented God's plan of salvation through the shed blood of Jesus Christ—all this in their own mother tongue in both scripts.

Since we had pulled up stakes in the Philippines, we no longer had a car there. Our plan, therefore, was to go to the coastal city of Iligan where we had lived for many years and hire a taxi to take us to the safety of the college campus in Marawi City. From there we would penetrate the lakeshore by public jeepneys. We reasoned that when a person was healed, even though a Muslim, he would not be so quick to harm us.

Before we discovered that there was no taxi driver on the island of Mindanao willing to risk his life or his car on a trip into that forbidden area, we visited with a young missionary couple from Canada, the Frenches, who had arrived in Iligan shortly before we left. Shocked that we would even consider the exposure of public transportation around the Lake, they handed us the keys to one of their cars. Missionaries don't normally have two cars, but the Frenches were in the process of selling this one, having recently purchased a larger vehicle. The car was God's miraculous provision, His seal of approval on this venture. Without wheels, we soon learned, we could have accomplished very little on the Lake and would have been exceedingly vulnerable to anyone who wished to harm us.

We left Iligan the next morning armed with our little tract and in our miracle car, which was packed with a two-week supply of food and water. We were thankful that the hotel on the university campus, where we had stayed thirty years earlier on our tract distribution trip, was still in operation. Being a government institution, Mindanao State University was heavily guarded by Filipino Marines, who also kept a watchful eye over the campus hotel, with its picturesque individual cottages.

Tugaya

Daily we made forays into the villages around the lakeshore. This was also reminiscent of that earlier tract distribution trip. On our third day we ventured as far as Tugaya, which, like the other barrios around the Lake, is located on its shores. The highway, however, leaves the Lake some distance before Tugaya and snakes high up around the mountain. The Marines had built their encampment at the very spot where the Tugaya road begins its descent to the Lake. When we asked them whether it would be safe for us to go down into Tugaya, they answered with raucous laughter, which meant they didn't think so. We sat down in the waiting shed on the highway to think and pray.

Soon three women got out of a public jeepney and joined us, amazed to hear us speak to them in Maranao. They were too hot and weary from a morning in town to walk the half-hour down to their homes, and so they waited for a passing car to give them a ride. Twice cars passed us on their way down to Tugaya without stopping for the women. Finally we decided it would be safe for us to go in the company of these Maranaos, who jumped at our offer to drive them down.

When we dropped off the last lady, we were almost at the lakeshore. As we made our way slowly back up the narrow, winding dirt road, scrutinizing each house, all of which had changed so much in the forty-five years since we had lived there, a strangely familiar one captured our attention. We stopped, our eyes riveted to the structure. The location was right, but it couldn't be "our" house because the entire front was cement. We decided to investigate, however, and as we got out of the car, a familiar looking young man approached us.

"Hello, Mr. and Mrs. Ward! And how is Greig? And

Carole? And Keith?" he said with outstretched hand and a broad smile. We were stunned! Our cover was blown!

"Maulana," we gasped. "Is this indeed where you live?"

He was our landlord's son, the second son of Hadji Abdullah, who had died some years earlier. His English was better now than when he was Greig and Keith's constant companion. He had forgotten only Sharon, who was a newborn when we left the Lake. The cement front of the house was an add-on, we learned.

But we were nervous that our identity was known. We were no longer American visitors studying Maranao at the university, as people naturally assumed. We were now seen as Christian missionaries, and what is worse, the very ones responsible for the Christian Bible in Maranao. Nevertheless, we stayed and chatted with Maulana and the other men who were sitting in the shed in the clearing.

I caught sight of one young man who was so clean-cut that he looked out of place, dressed as he was in Western style clothes, a young college student perhaps. I pictured him in my mind's eye as part of a campus ministry studying God's Word. He seemed interested in Bob's book, *So Sindaw.* He was so interested, in fact, that upon learning that this was the new *imam* of Tugaya, Bob gave him the Bible.

He had to be the youngest *imam* we had ever seen, only twenty-five years old, and certainly the least Muslim looking. Most *imams* and *ustads* try to look as much like Arabs as possible, wearing the long, white flowing robes and growing whatever beard their few whiskers will allow. Landua was his name. I wrote it down so that we could pray for him by name. The impact of what had happened didn't hit us until later. Bob had actually placed an entire Maranao Bible in the hands of an *imam* in Tugaya, our very first home in the Philippines. Even back then, Tugaya was one of the most fanatically Muslim centers of the entire Lake area and, in fact, throughout the Philippines. It still is.

Meanwhile, Maulana had distanced himself from the

group and was squatting with his back to us, using his cell phone. Suddenly we both jumped in the car and took off, burning rubber. We didn't know exactly why, we just knew we had to get out of there. Bob drove up the long steep hill with his foot hard against the floorboard. Later it occurred to us that Maulana was probably calling for someone to pick us up, most likely his older brother, Magasuga. Treachery was nothing new.

On our sixth day, after threats and warnings from people we chatted with along the highway, we realized we were being followed. We made it back into the heavily guarded university campus in the nick of time. Marines were everywhere. At our request the following morning, two of them escorted us down the mountain to the comparative safety of Iligan on the coast. How we would love to have stayed several more weeks on the Lake instead of six short days.

Before we left the Lake, however, we had placed another Bible in the hands of yet another *imam*, Hadji Mindosa, in a barrio closer to Marawi City. He was very eager to receive it, although he did not realize at the time that it was the Christian holy book. Our prayer is that both of these *imams*, so influential in their communities, will continue to study *So Sindaw* under the instruction of the Holy Spirit. Both of them are in strategic areas, and we trust that curiosity, at least, will keep them both reading and that the Holy Spirit will drive home to them the dynamite of God's Word.

After those six days on the Lake, the car we were driving was a marked vehicle and would not have been safe for anyone to drive. The Frenches sold it in the neighboring province where the airport is located, out of Muslim-controlled territory.

Our plan before we left was to pray for the sick everywhere, which we did. The Lord gave us the privilege of praying for eighteen people scattered in various barrios—a blind man, a polio cripple, an epileptic, and people with various other maladies, including a couple of young girls needing body parts. We returned to each sick person the following day and prayed again with unwavering faith, but none were healed, at least not before our eyes. We had fully expected to see the kind of results we had witnessed in the sixties when we prayed for terminally ill people, but this did not happen. God seemed to focus on penetrating the spiritual darkness of Islam with *So Sindaw*. After all, the ultimate goal of our trip was to bring the gospel to Maranaos, and the Holy Spirit reminded us, "My ways are not your ways."

We were not without miracles, of course. There was the miracle car. And the miracle of having placed a complete Bible in the hands of two *imams.* And there were the angels with the commission to accompany us wherever we went. They worked overtime to keep us safe and free for six whole days.

As Jesus reveals Himself today through dreams and visions to Muslims all over the world, He will surely not pass over the People of the Lake!

Chapter 15

Epilogue

Although we were "home" and based in Dallas, we were by no means retired. We had simply relocated, and we had two immediate objectives: to see *So Sindaw* posted on the Web and to transcribe it into the Arabic script.

The Web

Missionaries can no longer penetrate Lake Lanao, which is now completely closed behind the pale of Islam. In the third world, however, Internet cafés abound. The majority of people, too poor to own their own computer, can access the Internet for a fee so modest that even low incomes can afford it.

Through the kindness of our Wycliffe missionary friend, Dave, we now have a creative Web site where Maranaos can read the Bible in their mother tongue, safely ensconced in the privacy of an Internet café's computer booth.

The Arabic Script

The Koran is sacred to the Muslim, and a text printed in the Arabic script holds emotional value for Maranaos.

Throughout the Muslim provinces of the Philippines, children faithfully attend *madrasa* schools in the mosque on Friday and Saturday, where they are taught to sound out the Arabic letters from the Koran. No importance is placed on understanding, however, and they never grasp the meaning of the Arabic words which they are sounding out. Emphasis is placed entirely on reading smoothly from the Arabic Koran in preparation for Koran-reading contests, which are held annually throughout the Muslim world.

If they are reading Maranao words written with Arabic letters, and not Arabic words, every Maranao can understand them. And because the people are all taught to read the Arabic script, there are no illiterates on the Lake. The challenge, then, has been to transcribe *So Sindaw* into the Arabic letters. But this is easier said than done, because Maranaos have their own style of using the Arabic letters, a style which is peculiar to them.

Bob soon realized that his Arabic computer program would not enable him to finish the job in his lifetime. The Lord, however, sent help through Tom, an expert in Arabic, who wrote an incredibly helpful computer program tailored specifically for Maranao. It has speeded up the project by light-years. Even so, Bob still has to go over every word to make sure the letters conform to the way Maranaos write them.

Several books of the Maranao Bible in Arabic script have already been posted on the Web beside, *So Sindaw*. Who could have envisioned in 1961 such a thing as the Internet, especially as it is being used for the kingdom of God! Will you pray with us for the Light to shine and transform Maranao hearts?

Penetrating the Stronghold of Islam

To Contact the Author:

Bob and Mariel Ward
P. O. Box 535132
Grand Prairie, TX 75053

www.MarielWard.com

www.maranaonews.com